THE DIARY OF
WILLIAM YOUNG
OF COTCHFORD FARM

THE DIARY OF
WILLIAM YOUNG
OF COTCHFORD FARM

BY

KEVIN J. LAST

UNICORN

First published by Unicorn
an imprint of the Unicorn Publishing Group LLP, 2022
5 Newburgh Street
London W1F 7RG

www.unicornpublishing.org

The publisher has made every effort to contact the current copyright
holders to the pictures included in this book. Any omission is
unintentional, and the details should be addressed to Unicorn
Publishing Group to be rectified in any reprint.

10 9 8 7 6 5 4 3 2 1

ISBN 978-1-914414-29-9

CONTENTS

ILLUSTRATIONS

Cover: Cotchford Farm (PA Images/Alamy Stock Photo)

INTRODUCTION

THE BACKGROUND TO this book concerns Cotchford Farm in Hartfield, East Sussex, best known as the country home of Winnie-the-Pooh author A. A. Milne. While the latter is well known, there are other aspects to the history of this farmhouse which makes it a place of considerable interest and the key to some very different stories. This book does not pretend to be a complete account of the farm but, instead, of one of its owners; it shows how the house became a silent witness to periods of social change and defined the move from living for necessity to a life of work accompanied by a large measure of enjoyment.

The farmhouse lies to the south-west of Hartfield in the High Weald Area of Outstanding Natural Beauty. Originally timber-framed, the thatched roof was later replaced with tiles. It boasts an inglenook fireplace, a split-level drawing room, and, latterly, a swimming pool. It became a Grade II listed property in 1982. Its most recent sale, after some delay, was in June 2017, for £1.8 million. I visited the property on behalf of the BBC in January of that year. It was believed at one point to be wanted by the Disney organisation, but this was robustly opposed: just as well, as such a purchase would have been a disaster for that gentle Ashdown Forest area; the property would simply have been promoted for megabucks rather than for its history. Also the neighbourhood would most likely have been spoilt.

While the stories of two of its residents are very much public property, I became the unlikely and possibly the only source for the earliest account of the Farm, written in the middle of the nineteenth century. It is because of this – a diary that came into my hands by chance – that I decided to go public and then compare this story with later events. Cotchford Farm may have been a large, rambling home to some and a central player in a children's classic for others, but, over the years, it was also a place of hardship and, in one case, sudden death.

It has been about fifty years since I first listened to a vinyl record by the Rolling Stones called *Big Hits (High Tide and Green Grass)*. This iconoclastic group, apparently so critical of the world, were at the same time creating memories that its audience might keep in its collective mind as bookmarks of a certain period, both good and bad. I have always held the view that popular culture, like other types, even if appearing to be instantly dispensable, can create a stepladder of memories from various key points in our life that act as a sounding board to our inner self, coming, as they do, from aspects of art, literature, music, drama and film. But the Rolling Stones went one better than that. They created, in that abrasive fashion that only a significant band could manage, their own mystery. How did Brian Jones, the group's guitarist, come to die in the swimming pool at Cotchford Farm in 1969? In other words, did he jump or was he pushed? Of course, all such partly unexplained deaths create conspiracy theorists who mutter darkly of murky plotting. But, as we shall see, Brian Jones's death was not unique in the history of Cotchford Farm. It was simply another twist in the long history of this farmhouse, owned before A. A. Milne by the Young family, gentleman farmers in the nineteenth century. My intention, because I find myself in a unique position to do so, is to link these three very different stories, thus creating a context, and to show how they have altered our view of the site itself, ranging from the hard practicality of nineteenth-century farming, through a child's fantasy landscape, to a fallen idol.

Christopher Robin Milne (1920–1996) was very different from his father and from his fictional namesake, all of whom, nevertheless, shared a love of the countryside and its flora and fauna. Where A. A. Milne had acquired his under the fortunate tutelage of H. G. Wells, then a teacher at Henley House in Hampstead under the overall supervision of the head teacher – Milne's father – Christopher Robin learned his deep love of the countryside from the nearby Ashdown Forest and from his father's own books about Winnie-the-Pooh, published in 1924 and 1928. He was initially a spoilt child, brought up by a nanny who attended to his every need, but kept quite distant from his parents, as was often the case at the time in upper-middle-class households. This had the effect of leaving him with a lack of self confidence that lasted for a good part of his life, and a simmering resentment against his father, who he felt had abused him by making him a fictional character in his books; this had largely contributed to his father's success and financial security but, at the same time, had interfered with Christopher Robin's development. But Milne senior had suffered mentally from the anguish of the First World War, something I do not feel Christopher Robin ever really understood. But why should he? Such terrors would have been a mystery to a small boy. Alan Milne was both very competitive and, at the same time, emotionally distant from his son.

When Christopher grew up, studying at Stowe School and then Cambridge, he gradually became more certain of himself. His service in Africa and Italy during the Second World War initially got off to a poor start, but ultimately proved the making of him; despite a stammer, he became an expert on different types of mines. He was a responsible and caring junior officer, and although he did not expect to survive the war, his appreciation of the Italian countryside and his offbeat observations got him through it relatively unscathed, apart from a shrapnel wound from which he made a full recovery.

This did not stop him having a hard time in London after the war, initially at John Lewis. While he was capable of simple carpentry, he was not at all on the wavelength of this up-market but somewhat claustrophobic store from which he was eventually sacked. He just needed a job and, despite his war service, something suitable for a Cambridge man seemed hard to come by. He did find his wonderful wife there, Leslie de Selincourt, a relation of his mother's, who brought him back from the brink. It was almost a case of history repeating itself, with both father and son marrying into the same family. Together they answered an advertisement and opened The Harbour Bookshop in Dartmouth in 1950. Living initially above the shop and then separately in a house where they could both enjoy the countryside, their home became a haven for their cats and other animals. Christopher spent many happy years with his wife, eventually looking after his disabled daughter, Clare. To ensure her future he, perhaps unwisely, sold the rights to the Pooh books. It was not a desire for money that motivated him but the necessity of ensuring the necessary care for his daughter. Christopher was a mild man, relatively unambitious but keen to do well by his family.

While Christopher learned much from his father, he remained somewhat estranged from his parents for the rest of their lives. Cotchford and Ashdown Forest (posing as Hundred Acre Wood) taught him much about natural history, as it did for many small children after the war, a salutary lesson to today's media-driven young people. A piece of 1929 archive film depicts Christopher in Ashdown Forest with other children dressed as his father's animals. That seems a delightful way to remember him. His love of the land and its animals was remarkable and something the modern generation seems to have forgotten. And when the summer sun sets on Galleon's Lap (Gills Lap) in Hundred Acre Wood, I would like to imagine his ghost still flitting silently among the trees.

Brian Lewis Hopkin-Jones was a very different animal. Brian came from a middle-class background in Cheltenham. He was born in 1942, the son of Welsh aeronautical engineer Lewis Blount Jones and his wife, Louisa. Life started badly with the death of his baby sister, Pauline, to leukaemia when he was just four. His parents failed to share their grief with him and so, from an early age, he felt an outsider. Tremendously talented but fundamentally lazy and undisciplined, Brian could have been anything he wanted. He could pass exams relatively easily and was able to play virtually any instrument he picked up. His father had visions of him as a dentist or even as a classical pianist, but it was not to be. Brian started down a different road, fascinated by the swinging music he heard in the coffee bars that were beginning to invade stuffy old post-war Cheltenham. Yet there was another surprising side of Brian Jones which we should not forget. He avidly read the Bible throughout his life, as if looking for an anchor against his increasingly wild escapades. Nevertheless he got a fourteen-year-old girl, Valerie, in the family way and was exiled to Germany for two weeks in a vain attempt to hush it up. Abortion was talked about but eventually the child was put up for adoption, the first of five illegitimate children in Jones's very short life. Ostracised by the burghers of Cheltenham and his parents, Brian withdrew into himself but found a way forward in his musical ability that led eventually to his formation of the Rolling Stones.

This led to a wild and claustrophobic life in what was probably the golden era of popular music. It meant being constantly on the road, living in cheap digs and hotel bedrooms, and a never-ending run of alcohol, drugs and loose women. In the early days the Stones did not make a great deal of money. They were not commercial enough and their wild behaviour was only one of many problems. The apparent solution to their difficulties arrived in the form of Tom Keylock, an ex-army man who was as tough he needed to be and a good organiser; he kept the band in shape for whatever venue they attended. But he was also the key to Brian Jones's demise when the Stones' founder decided he had had enough of the hassle of being constantly on the road and had found a country retreat in the form of Cotchford Farm. When Jones wanted to renovate it, Keylock put him in touch with the shady Frank Thorogood, a disreputable and incompetent East End builder, who moved in with his mates and began to make Jones's life a misery. Thorogood stole cash that Jones had carelessly left lying around and, along with his cronies, drank him dry. He never properly undertook the work required, despite taking payment. While Keylock was in most respects efficient, it is something of a mystery why he thought Thorogood was an appropriate choice. He had already blotted his copybook with work at Keith Richards' house.

In the meantime, Mick Jagger and the other members of the Stones were looking for a more commercial sound and decided that Jones, who was proving increasingly unreliable, was no longer required. He had been had up several times for drug use and, for that reason, could not go on an American tour. Neither, despite his musical skills, had he produced any worthwhile songs. Therefore, in June 1969, Jagger and Richards arrived at Cotchford and informed Jones he had been sacked. He had been half expecting it and was left with a financial settlement and the use of the Stones' office facilities. In an ironic turnaround the founder of this iconic group had been summarily dismissed by the band members he'd recruited in the first place.

Brian Jones appeared to recover from this, tentatively aligning himself with other artists, but Thorogood kept up the heat on him; on 3 July 1969, after a drunken evening swim, Jones was found dead at the bottom of the Cotchford swimming pool. There was a cover-up, but it seems likely that Thorogood, concerned that he might lose his position, may have held Jones, an asthmatic, underwater for too long. This was never proved or properly investigated but, according to Keylock, Thorogood admitted to him privately on his deathbed in hospital that he had done for Jones.

The house – originally the site of a sixteenth-century crown forge – is not particularly beautiful, having been subject to many changes over the centuries. But now its association with 'a bear of very little brain' has ensured an audience and a focal point for a child's imagination thanks to the pen of A. A. Milne and the enchanting drawings of E. H. Shepard. This magical combination represents the music and lyrics, as it were, of that very special land of childhood and discovery. Bookending Milne's works were the contrasting harshness of two world wars and I found myself in the strange position of being the only person holding the key to one part of its incredible early history.

The sundial in Cotchford's garden bears the words, 'This warm and sunny spot belongs to Pooh. And here he wonders what it's time to do.' This was also an apt description for Pooh lookalike Brian Jones with his blond mop and short stature. The stream that runs along the garden's southern boundary eventually leads to the

Poohsticks Bridge, half a mile distant. A special place that was briefly turned into a nightmare.

What I have outlined is a brief history of the highlights of the twentieth-century history of Cotchford Farm. But this book concerns an earlier period, when Cotchford was a working farm rather than a country house, as we turn the clock back to the mid-nineteenth century for another remarkable story.

DISCLAIMER

I am by training a film historian. I took up this work as a project because it was too good to throw up because of a personal connection. It is possible, therefore, that I have failed to interpret correctly or misunderstood aspects of farming, mill work, stone dressing and social history references. If that is the case I can only apologise. The fault is all mine.

DISCOVERY

M Y MOTHER'S FAMILY came from generally humble stock although one or two ancestors did quite well for themselves. Sir J. W. Redhouse (1811–92), a high-flying diplomat, produced the first *English and Turkish Dictionary* (1857), yet current volumes do not even credit him, while still using the name Redhouse to describe the dictionary. I was fortunate to have found an original in a bookshop at Hay-on-Wye.

More recently, since the 1960s, I had an aunt, Mary Belton, my mother's sister, who always seemed to be bumping along the bottom of life's escalator, ever dependent on other people to keep her afloat. Her father at one time ran an early example of a low-rent holiday camp for displaced youths in Shoreham, outside Brighton. It is even possible that Billy Butlin, the holiday camp entrepreneur, got the idea from this enterprise. He was supposed to have visited.

My aunt lived almost all her life in Brighton, eventually marrying a central heating engineer who, far from keeping her warm and comfortable, instead decided to die remarkably young. This meant that her relatively slender means became even slenderer, and there were regular calls for handouts, most notably from my mother, who I have to say always responded to these requests, albeit without a great deal of enthusiasm. Regular trips were made from London to Brighton, often via the Brighton Belle Pullman, which made up for with beauty what it lacked in good springing.

The first time I encountered my aunt was in one of those narrow-terraced cottages in Brighton full of dark curtains and very

Mary Belton skating in Brighton c.1935

little daylight. It even had an outside privy. Apart from my aunt, the property was occupied by a number of cats who she loved as family and who seemed to know they were on to a good thing by learning how to transfer from room to room by swinging on the door handles.

My aunt was a person of little ambition, although I had a photograph of her as an apparently competent ice skater which perhaps, in an early lifetime not beset with social stigma and war, might have led to an entirely different and more satisfactory existence. She was a creature of Brighton's Lanes and antique shops, and it was the latter that brought about the possibility of this book. Even when I got to know her better in later life she still had a few interesting items such as mementos of closed cinemas and rare volumes on silent film. She particularly loved the sea and its suggestion of adventure, its moods and its secrets, although, as far as I know, she never ventured abroad.

I lived some considerable distance away but I made a point of visiting her twice a year in her old age. When my mother found herself with a form of cancer in 1995 and soon after died, she left me a letter requesting me to keep an eye on my aunt, now around eighty-three but still smoking like a chimney. She lived at that time in a flat in North Road, Brighton; until relatively recently she had made a living repairing pianolas, which kept her busy following the early and entirely unexpected death of her husband. Despite that skill, she was not an able businesswoman and was frequently taken advantage of financially. She was once caught up in a near riot at the local port in Shoreham where a container ship full of livestock was travelling in dire conditions.

When eventually she was turfed out of the flat so that developers could cash in on a redevelopment scheme, there was initially nowhere for her to go. A relative offered her the use of a bungalow inland for the duration but she declined, preferring to be nearer the sea. As she grew steadily frailer, local relatives arranged for her to be admitted to a local residential home in Hove where she lived out the rest of her days, apparently none the worse for her steady intake of tobacco. When she was no longer mobile, she took a simple pleasure in watching the seagulls landing on the nearby rooftops from her room, seeing perhaps what she was lacking in their mobility and freedom.

I found these visits a bit of a struggle. Her early background of relative poverty was very different to mine, growing up in the stockbroker belt north-west of London. I didn't really have much in common with my aunt, but my wife and I did our best to make these visits enjoyable, occasionally taking her out for short walks in the local neighbourhood of the town where she had spent practically her entire life. 'I can still run!' she said, but she couldn't. 'I hate old people,' she said, never seemingly recognising that she herself was now old and not above being a bit of a thorn in the side of the wonderful staff who tried to look after their motley charges, even taking them on outings for a change of surroundings. This was above the call of duty. She eventually passed away at the age of ninety-eight, not apparently having achieved anything very notable other than a lifelong support for animals in distress, and the possession of some interesting artefacts.

There was, however, to be a silver lining. When my aunt moved out of her flat, she had to dispose of a number of possessions, including books about film and a couple of ancient but seemingly unremarkable exercise books filled with closely written handwriting. At first I took very little notice, not considering them of any value, film being my area of expertise. There was a rare volume on the history of silent movies, and it was some time before I turned to the exercise books.

One was remarkable, being a record of early mathematical calculations, beautifully laid out, from sometime in the nineteenth century. These exercises could set an example to many a careless modern student some 200 years later in terms of their exactness. Such discipline! The other, however, was different again, except in its precision, being a closely written account of a young farmworker in the mid-nineteenth century, William Young, who left Scotsford Farm in Hartfield, East Sussex, travelled by train to London and then Liverpool, before taking a ship across the Atlantic. His destination was the saw and flour mills on the Canadian Great Lakes. On closer inspection the diary could not have been the work of a labourer. It was too well written and precise. No, our man had received a reasonable education for the time and had, perhaps by force of circumstance, been compelled to make the appalling wrench from what must have been a relatively comfortable existence in nineteenth-century Sussex to an unknown and possibly hostile environment across the Atlantic. That must have taken courage and resourcefulness. I was immediately struck by his determination and how, despite being only twenty-three, he had kept his eye on the target at all times. I will now examine the background to this young man's departure from what seemed an assured home life.

THE FARMING REVOLUTION

A S TO WHY our diarist took this trip, we need only to look at the history of agriculture in the mid-nineteenth century to realise that this was the beginning of a severe contraction of the number of people who worked on the land due to the modernisation of farming methods: just another aspect of the huge transformation that the country underwent as a result of the Industrial Revolution. Increased size and mechanisation may have improved farms' profits and made them easier to manage, but the obverse of that coin was the number of farmworkers put out of a job as a result. Our man may have been one such casualty, and while the diary is important for a number of reasons, it is also a first-hand account of one person's ability to deal with this problem. Unlike many other redundant workers at this time who were left in poverty, the diarist had some money. He came from a relatively secure family background. But who was he and what was his connection to Cotchford Farm?

According to the first page of the diary, William Young left Scotsford Farm on 24 June 1854 to take a train to London. His family must have wondered if they would ever see him again. William, according to the 1841 census, was the eldest son of farmer Henry Young. Henry had a wife and daughter, both called Orpha (sometimes spelt Oprah), and a younger son called Thomas. Orpha, the daughter, possibly William's twin, is referred to as Fanny in the diary. There were also four servants and a young boy called James Fuller. So, quite a number of mouths to feed, and it must have been a blow to Henry Young when William, his eldest, announced his journey. Perhaps his departure eased the family finances. By the 1851 census, William and Thomas had disappeared and been replaced by Spencer, William's younger brother.

Did William go because he realised there would not be enough work to maintain him for much longer, or was there another reason? We can't know for sure, but the first explanation is the most likely and in line with the reduction in agricultural workers at that time. Strip-field farming may have previously kept the locals in work, but it was no longer an economical way to run a farm.

We might imagine that it is only in today's technological age that change takes place so fast. Surprisingly, this was just as true in the nineteenth century in terms of changes in agricultural development; this may hold the key to William Young's decision to leave home in 1854 and make his way to the other side of the world. Although many workers were in the same position, few of them had the money or the perseverance to go abroad and seek new opportunities. It is also possible William moved abroad in search of knowledge, hoping to use the modern methods he would learn overseas to assist the community at home in England. Alternatively, it could be seen as a kind of 'gap year' in modern parlance.

I will outline here some of farming's major improvements at that time, leading to an increase in crop yield but a inevitable downturn in the number of people who worked on the land. This was something always regretted by the writer D.H. Lawrence, who felt that those in touch with the land had a uniquely special understanding of nature and the meaning of life.

Amongst the new developments was the Norfolk four-course crop rotation, basically meaning that a cycle of fallow land was replaced by the growth of root crops like turnips and other crops such as clover. This was a way of maximising field usage.

The Dutch and Rotherham swing and wheelless plough, which required fewer oxen or horses, superseded the basic Chinese plough.

A national market also developed, free of tariffs, custom barriers and tolls. Transportation improved both in terms of roads and the introduction of railways. Land was converted into more easily managed units with better drainage; in some places land was reclaimed from the sea and from areas choked with bracken and nettles. Greater expertise in selective breeding created greater uniformity of quality in livestock.

While all these improvements were likely to reduce the number of workers required, none had a greater effect than the introduction of enclosures. Up until recently, in contemporary terms, farming was still following to a greater or lesser extent the medieval open field system whereby subsistence farmers worked strips of land under the auspices of the landowner, often the aristocracy or, before that, the Catholic Church. The introduction of enclosures and the ensuing disintegration of the early feudal system had begun as early as 1350, from bitter necessity due to a depleted population after the Black Death in 1348. This process eventually accelerated, as the land could be serviced more efficiently by fewer people over larger field systems. This resulted in fewer farmers and the creation of a new class of poor who had lost the means for even basic subsistence farming. Some managed to find other jobs at home, while others, like William Young, went abroad to find work. The effect of the enclosures was devastating but essential for the economic development of modern farming. While this process was largely complete by the end of the eighteenth century, the continuing improvements outlined above, amongst others, meant agricultural workers were still being laid off in the nineteenth century.

I had one major query to solve in the diary: was Scotsford Farm the same place as Cotchford Farm? Hartfield is not a big place and I hoped that a census would provide the necessary information. Fortunately the 1841 census came to the rescue, listing farmer Henry Young's entire household in June of that year. The only curiosity was the inclusion of an eleven-year-old boy, James Fuller, of whom it says simply 'born Sussex'. He appears to have no relation to either the family or the servants. While apparently not relevant to this story, his inclusion remains a curiosity.

According to Charles Nassau Sutton (1902), the first mention of Cotchford (or Cottesford) Farm is in a list of jurymen (1265) when an inquest was held concerning the Rebels of Sussex after the Barons War. Amongst the names shown is William Cotchford (p.347).

A few centuries later we come to William Cotchford (alias Cotchforde or Scotchford) in the late 1500s. Amusingly, he crops up again in an action between Elizabeth Tyrre and his wife, Margery, when he has to pay £10, a sizeable sum in those days, to ensure that his wife keeps the peace between the two women, probably in 1596 (Kent History and Library Centre). His death occurred in 1619 so he lived around the same time as Shakespeare. From the above we can see why the farm, now reverted to its original name, was for a time known as Scotsford during the period of our diarist and that the further we go back, the less certain are the spellings. In 1656, the farm appears to have started life as a crown forge, then perhaps known as Cottesford (Sutton, p.309).

It is not a particularly pretty building nor even, dare one say it, a comfortable one, having been much modified and added to over the years but its panelled dining room offers a clue to its status as having an important place in social history. At the time of writing, it has recently been sold but it took some time, illustrating that having an interesting house with substantial history is not always a unique selling point. It has always seemed to me that it became established in the public mind not because of what it looked like but because of what happened there and its establishment as a gateway to a child's fantasy world.

I have attached some pages from the diary as an appendix to this book; it is interesting how practical and disciplined it is, and how precise a picture it gives of a young man on such a brave journey thousands of miles across the Atlantic. It is factual and remarkably free of emotion. It must have been an incredible wrench for a farmer's young son to leave the bosom of his family. It is a little disappointing that the diary provides few clues as to what this move to a new continent – not long before the American Civil War (1861–1865) – meant to William emotionally, but he obviously gained many new skills. We can only surmise from the evidence that such a focused person is likely to have been a credit to whoever employed him.

It is this down-to-earth aspect that connects him with A. A. Milne, as we shall see, whose fiction of an idyllic childhood in Ashdown Forest with its concentration on the land was at odds with the mental suffering that it seems to have caused his son, Christopher Robin. In view of this, Cotchford Farm may be regarded as a romantic place, but in many ways it had previously been a practical and a tough site, starting life as a crown forge before becoming a farm and then a country retreat. In fact, its layout, with many changes and additions over the years, meant that it always would have been hard to manage. Certainly, farming in Hartfield in the mid-nineteenth century, without the benefit of modern methods and machinery, was no easy task. People of the twenty-first century take it for granted they will have plenty of downtime and leisure time. But 200 years ago, life for agricultural workers and servants was an endless round of chores.

The population of Great Britain more than tripled between 1801 and 1901, from eleven million to thirty-seven million; these people had to be clothed and fed efficiently. This helps us understand the need for huge economic improvements in farming practices, including artificial fertilisers to work alongside the organic ones, such as potash and super phosphate, involving fossils dissolved in sulphuric acid. There was also a major improvement in seed planting, previously thrown by hand and gently harrowed. In 1701 when Jethro Tull refined a seed drill, which originated from China via Venice. This was a mechanical seeder which spread the seeds on a plot of land at the correct depth. But while it took away some of the laborious and wasteful nature of hand sowing, Tull's invention proved rather unreliable until better quality seed drills were introduced in the mid-eighteenth century.

All of the above provides a background to and possible reasons for the departure of William Young from Hartfield in 1854 to Canada via London and Liverpool. In the next section I want to look in detail at the nature of the diary itself.

THE DIARY

WILLIAM YOUNG HIMSELF would be amazed to know that his diary, written over 165 years ago, has survived to the present day. He obviously never intended it for publication and yet it gives a voice to a young man apparently determined to overcome the difficulties of agricultural life in the mid-nineteenth century, providing a first-hand living history. It is a shame we have no picture of him.

The diary initially seems disappointing because it was written in a remarkably impersonal tone, almost free of emotion and concentrating on the facts of everyday life. However, it does provide a very objective view of the events he experienced. Only later, when he is aboard ship and arriving in Canada, does the sense of amazement of visiting a new and strange continent begin to infuse the diary. And yet if one were to give such a project to a student, it would achieve high marks as an incredibly clear and concise account of a personal journey lasting just over a year.

Using the first page as an example, the account of Young's departure is utterly straightforward, detailed and unsentimental:

Wednesday 29th June, 1854. Started from Scotsford at a quarter past six o'oclock at and arrived at Edenbridge at half past seven. Train started for London at a quarter past eight. It rained all the way from Hartfield.

What a miserable departure from the family home on a wet midsummer day! And yet there is no evidence of regret or worry at the start of this huge undertaking. William Young must have wondered at the task ahead of him. Yet what shines through this first page and indeed the entire diary is his determination to succeed.

The other characteristic that comes through from this first page is the precision about money and the need to account for it:

Paid two and seven from Edenbridge to London Bridge... Paid for fare of sixteen and nine by third class passage [from London Euston to Liverpool].

This is a very careful and well organised young man. And yet, all this trauma does seem to have had an effect although we are spared the details:

1854. 2nd [July]. Sunday. Very poorly all day. Walked a little in the evening. 3rd. A great deal worse and laid down nearly all day. Took some medicine and got better towards evening.

But it is not all doom and gloom. Young tells us how he:

Walked round the docks [in Liverpool] and saw very little except sailors and girls. 3rd [July]. Went to the Parisian gallery of Anatomy [a strange choice!]. Saw 300 anatomical models and heard a good lecture and learnt much.

All the way through the diary are examples of an analytical and enquiring mind:

4th [July]. Afternoon. Went to the zoological gardens. Saw the circus, theatre and fireworks display and thought it very good.

Of course, Young had next to find a ship. It is not clear whether he had planned this in advance, but he used his spare time between arriving in Liverpool and boarding his ship *The William Tapscott*. Unbeknownst to him, Young was taking considerable risks in his choice of passage.

The William Tapscott was built in 1852 by William Drummond at Bath, Maine. It had weighed 1,525 tons, and was 195 feet long and 41 feet wide. *The William Tapscott* was one of the largest full-rigged ships built in Maine during the 1850s. According to the Mormon Immigration Index 'she was a typical "Down Easter" – sturdy, moneymaking, moderately sparred, and designed for carrying capacity. She was a three-decker with a square stem and billethead.' The key word here is 'moneymaking', as we shall see. Even so, *The William Tapscott*, when in full sail, must have made an impressive sight.

Shortly after Young's journey, the ship was chartered by the Mormon church to return missionaries and converts from Liverpool to New York. She left Liverpool on 11 April 1859 and arrived in New York on 13 May 1859. This was a relatively harmonious voyage but, later, tragedy hit this ill-starred vessel.

LIVERPOOL TO
THE NEW WORLD

O N THE AFTERNOON of 5 July, Young visited the ship's office and secured a berth in No. 44, the second cabin for which pays five £10 notes. It seems that passengers on board the vessel had very much to fend for themselves because on 7 July, Young tells us how he 'Went and bought some provisions at Tapscott and a bed barrel. Paid £12.12s.2p for them.'

It is worth pointing out that this was a time of substantial emigration, not just from England and not just because of agricultural changes. These ships also acted as a means of passage from other parts of Europe, particularly Scandinavia, to the New World, which was gradually opening up for the bravest travellers.

Young's choice of ship had a chequered history, as Erin M. McGreevy tells us:

In the pre-Famine era, many Irish boarded cargo ships in order to emigrate to the United States, Canada, and other countries. At their best, these sea voyages were uncomfortable; at their worst, perilous. The passengers who were not wealthy travellers were assigned berths in cramped quarters 'tween decks or in steerage, often literally on top of other people.

Disease was also a concern, especially considering ship board conditions were not sanitary due to human waste and the close proximity to sick passengers or to those carrying disease, such as cholera. Food and water were scarce; passengers were often forced to consume uncooked or spoiled food or face starvation.

Additionally, the season and weather conditions could prove to be disastrous. A winter voyage could lead to freezing temperature and hypothermia, while mid-summer journeys could bring dehydration and dangerously hot temperatures in the cramped decks and quarters. (2017)

William Young's voyage seemed less hazardous than some of the other accounts of passengers on this ship (one tells of a fire on board), but he does tell us that on 11 July, before they had even set sail, while still in the river near the docks:

'A man fell overboard. The boats were lowered immediately but the tide was running very fast. He was driven about ½ mile before he was rescued. He was taken on board again and seemed all right.'

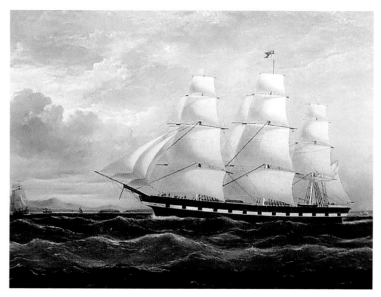

The William Tapscott, a three-masted schooner

The name of the ship originated with its owners. William Tapscott almost certainly came from a family who lived in Minehead, Somerset in the mid 1700s. William was an American packet ship broker, with offices on Regents Road, Liverpool, and Eden Quay, Dublin. Working with brother James, based in New York, they specialised in selling prepaid passages to bona fide immigrants, sometimes in large numbers, like the Mormons for example.

The Tapscott brothers were also agents for other packet ship groups such as the Black Ball Line.

Together, they fleeced the unsuspecting and were systematic villains on a grand scale. Their frauds began with their advertisements. Tapscott advertised that most of his ships were over 1,000 tons, with some over 2,000. In truth, most weighed barely 600 tons and were therefore at risk from the Atlantic gales. *The Garrick*, for example was said to be 2,000 tons, whereas it was actually only 895! *The William Tapscott* was advertised as weighing 3,000 tons, but was under 2,000. They claimed to be cargo ships and, while this was true to some extent, their cargo was often human. An advertisement of the day claimed, 'The above ships are of the largest class, commanded by men of experience, who will take every precaution to promote the health and comfort of the passengers during the voyage.' (TheShipsList, 2018).

This was a long way from the truth as conditions were often terrible: food was poor (corn grits) and there was an insufficient supply of water. The passengers were certainly treated like cargo, but they were not the only ones to be taken advantage of: William Tapscott played fast and loose with the shareholders' money. Eventually he was convicted for fraud and false accounting and sentenced to three years' penal servitude.

The following windlass shanty would be sung by the men while the ship was being warped out of harbour on a long rope attached to the windlass (a winch). A rope would be made fast to a quayside ring, run round a bollard at the pier head and then back to the ship's windlass. So-called 'spokesters' would attempt to turn the winch while the men sang. The mechanism of the winch had something in common with the opening of a canal lock gate.

TAPSCOTT (We're All Bound to Go)

As I walked out one morning, all down the Clarence Dock,
Heave away, aye, me Johnnies! Heave away!
Twas there I spied an Irish girl conversing with Tapscott.
And away my Johnny boys! We're all bound to go!

'Good morning, Mr Tapscott.' 'Good morning, my dear,' says he.
Heave away, aye, me Johnnies! Heave away!
'Oh do you have a packet ship to bear me over the seas?'
And away my Johnny boys! We're all bound to go!

'Oh, yes, I have a packet ship. She's a packet of note and fame.
She's lying at the Waterloo Dock and Henry Clay's *her name.'*

'Bad luck unto the Henry Clay *and the day that she set sail.*
For them sailors got drunk and broke into my bunk and they
*   stole my clothes away.'*

'Twas at the Castle Garden they landed me ashore
And if I marry a Yankee boy I'll sail the seas no more.'

The first part of this shanty reads like a satirical take on an advertisement, while the second shows the risks of such a voyage, particularly for young women.

Things did not end well for the ship either. *The William Tapscott* was wrecked on the rocks offshore at Bude on the north Cornwall coast in March 1888 whilst travelling from Mexico to Cardiff. Her figurehead was salvaged and can now be seen in the Bude museum. I have examined it recently. It is probably from the ship's office, not the bow, and looks like something you wish you had not won at an old fashioned fair.

A fitting end perhaps to a dodgy enterprise. The Bude coastal authorities were highly organised, being used to ships coming to grief on the ships offshore. As a result they had a rocket launcher with a line which, when it landed aboard, could be used as a rescue for the crew members to find their way ashore. In the case of *The William Tapscott* the entire crew was rescued although the ship was done for. Only a dog was drowned. The captain, left the ship's log and some valuable instruments that he had been meaning to take ashore, in his cabin. Its cargo of granite was thought lost but many years later in the 1930s it came to light, was recovered and used as a basis for the footpaths around Bude. An early example of recycling perhaps!

Despite being summer, the weather on Young's voyage was, as might be expected in the Atlantic, variable. Young gives a very clear picture of what it was like. There had not been many developments at sea in hundreds of years in terms of wooden ships, but all was about to change with the coming of Brunel and others:

18th July. Very strong wind and rough sea. A heavy gale came on about noon. Took the sails in and the ship tossed and turned very much. The women were frightened very much, some a crying and some a praying. Gale continued until 4 o'clock on the 19th.

Therefore the ship, now effectively without power, was at the mercy of the storm. But Young was remarkably relaxed:

I wanted to see once in my life a storm at sea and no life or damage done. The captain was afraid of the masts falling. A restless night. It cured the seasickness!

When William Young set sail in 1854, *The William Tapscott* was relatively new, having only been commissioned in 1852. However, because she was principally a cargo ship, she was only able to take passengers under fairly basic conditions. The crew were often as rough as the crossing, and the passengers' treatment was a million miles away from that expected by passengers on cruise ships today. You booked your passage and you took your chances, mostly fending for yourself. But Young, of course, would not have known what to expect, but he does make this comment:

22nd July. Rose early and began [to] serve the flour out to the passengers upwards of 900 lots and saw with disgust the imposition that was practised with them in all the provisions and water by the steward.

This was little better than prison rations. The restricted supply of such basics as water was to become a regular problem on board, only relaxing as they approached New York.

While Young appears to be very sanguine about the conditions, he does provide one small clue to the ship's extraordinary history, the problems simmering below the surface which led to her eventual wrecking off Bude:

9th July. The Wesleyan who was most zealous in his religion, recovered some water that his companion (another rank Wesleyan) had stolen from his shipmates and they jointly used it well knowing it to have been stolen.

10th. My companion Wright Stanley complains of the short quantity of water issued on which the steward struck him. He returned the blow. Consequently a sharp fight ensued but Mr Jones, the number 2, parted them.

Young goes on to tell how:

...the mates threw some bucketts [sic] of water in the crowds to disperse them, which had in some degree the desired effect, but they assembled again.

This may not seem other than a relatively trivial matter, but it provides a clue to the sparse conditions endured by those who undertook this voyage as passengers. In 1873 it led to an extraordinary and relatively little-known mutiny:

The master of the ship, James Cunningham Flynn, shared details of the mutinous event when the ship was forced to dock in Wellington, New Zealand on July 25, 1873 under the direction of the chief officer, Bernard King. According to Flynn, the crew and the captain had disagreements about the seaworthiness of the ship and the brutality of the captain. The crew declared the ship 'rotten and falling to pieces' and unfit to go around Cape Horn. The captain planned to dock at St. Helena [where Napoleon was held in 1815], much of their journey completed but the crew was not satisfied with this choice. Once the captain decided he would not make an *intermediate stop on the over 25,000 mile journey, the crew mutinied and violence broke out on the ship. The mate fired on the captain [in the knee] and the captain attacked the crew with an axe, declaring he would cut off the head or hand of any man who came near him. The mutiny ended with the captain being placed in irons in his cabin. There is no record of any passengers being injured, but a violent event like this taking place on a ship with passengers braving a long journey across the ocean would only put them in more danger than they already face on a cargo liner in the mid to late-1800s. Considering there were recorded animosity and harassment of steerage passengers at the hands of the ship mates, this is a terrifying situation to be trapped in. A mutiny on board and a captain restrained could have meant death for innocent passengers and never arriving at your final destination: America.*(McGreevy, 2017)*

At the time of Young's voyage, however, the ship was only two years old. On 23 July 1854, a fine and rather warm Sunday, Young reports that there is 'nothing to be seen but a whale'.

Interestingly, when one considers how the ship was also used for the transfer of Mormons to the New World, Young tells us that there was:

No divine service of any kind. Passengers did not dress up to keep the day at all separate from any other day.

This must have been a surprise given the apparent formality of the Victorian era. But, of course, the William Tapscott was an American ship from a considerably less than pedigree background and took passengers, including Mormons, whenever the Tapscotts saw a chance to make money. The conditions on board were therefore absolutely basic, perhaps matching the frontier conditions in parts of America and creating the growing tensions that would lead to the Civil War. Yet despite these problems Young seemed determined to enjoy himself:

26th July. A favorable [sic] wind all day. Went about 200 miles in a day and night. I have had a good appetite and enjoyed myself much. It was beautiful and starlight all night. I was on deck to 12 o'clock. I was very happy.

Eventually the first small signs of the New World became apparent:

30th July. A little wind in the morning... carried us on the banks of Newfound land and about 150 miles from the Island saw one land bird on the rigging of the vessel. The first one that has been seen since we left land and about the size of a sparrow and apparently of that species.

As so often, the area was covered in fog all day and the ship's bell was rung about every five minutes.

The next day Young saw about twenty Newfoundland fishing boats, three of which were close. But then he made a rather odd report:

I had a hard pain in my side. It lasted about 2 hours. Several more of the passengers had a similar pain.

Young offers no explanation for this strange and multiple occurrence. It was almost literally a sharp awakening to the New World.

While William Young seems to have been able to take most of what happened to him in his stride, it was no doubt a relief to be close to New York and at the end of an arduous and potentially dangerous voyage. In those days immigrants landed directly at the docks.

NEW YORK, NEW YORK!

O N 12 AUGUST, Young reported seeing the pilot boat with his glass; the pilot came on board at half past one:

A few hours a great deal of singing on board and nearly all the passengers stayed up all night in expectation of seeing land at break of day.

On 5 August, Young tells us how he:

...heard the best discussion between the Unitarians and the Wesleyans that I ever heard. Saw the sun set. It surpassed any thing of thousands I ever saw in England.

This comment emphasises the religious aspect of the ship's passengers, despite the nature of her owners. It crops up again later in the diary.

On 13 August Young describes how the:

Heracles tug boat came alongside. After haggling half an hour, agreed to take us in tow for 120 dollars. Sandy Hook was the first land that was seen and as we passed it the view was beautiful.

The end of the voyage was in sight and:

Early in the morning several tug boats came in search of a job. At

8.0am the Heracles came and took us up the North River to the quarantine ground and the doctor came on board but it was a mere form again and about 20 male (sic) boats came with the well known York runners and frightened some of the unprotected females.

Young goes on to give an account of the quarantine arrangements:

Statten [sic] Island is a beautiful place [!] with an hospital for all sorts of diseased emigrants although some vessels were compelled to remain in the quarantine ground on account of the illness on board.

In some ways the treatment of the immigrants seems remarkably similar to our own time with quite stringent checks taking place:

The customs house officers examined our luggage as we took it from the ship to the steam boat. They only opened about ½ of all the packages they pass. They pass mine without looking at it. Them that they open they only put there [sic] hand down at the side of the contents and turned a few of them up.

From 1855, immigrants landed at Castle Garden, New York, but this was a year before that clearing station opened. Ellis Island was used from 1890. Castle Garden was a small island just off Manhattan, very near the location of the Twin Towers which were destroyed by terrorists in 2001. It is known today as Fort Clinton, after the former New York Governor DeWitt Clinton. It is a circular stone structure with cannon ports around it, providing potential protection for the city. Landfill from excavations for buildings in New York was dumped between the two islands in modern times, joining them together. Immigrants disembarked

View from Staten Island, New York c.1855

and were processed at Castle Garden. They had to be cleared medically and financially to be permitted to leave.

But for Young, New York was only a way station for Canada. Passengers seemed to face similar ticketing difficulties to modern travellers:

Passengers should not book themselves to there (sic) *destination when they are at Liverpool as they will find some difficulty in going through should there destination be beyond Dimchurch or Buffalo as the Erie Company does not extend further. After our luggage was safely put in the depot of the Erie Company and we had taken our ticket by the emigrant tram to different places, to Buffalo or*

Dimchurch 4 dollars. The tickets are good until the end of the year on which they are issued.

Young describes:

...how we then went to different hotels and boarding houses but most of us went to the Fountain kept by Mr Hinton not far from the office of the Erie Company. Although the accommodation was not very good, there [sic] charge for board and lodging and the lodgings were very bad.

Quite apart from the fact that Young was a migrant and therefore low in the pecking order, immigrants had to be very careful of tricksters who tried to take advantage of them. Affordable lodgings were available for newly arrived immigrants in New York, but the unsuspecting would often be lured to much more expensive accommodation in the city centre. This was one of the reasons why Castle Garden was subsequently opened, to reduce the likelihood of this scamming.

It is very difficult to get good accommodation in New York at anything like reasonable charges.'

This was an expensive city even then. Young tells how, to get away from his awful lodgings for a while, he and his companions walked to Broadway in the evening. Young may perhaps have questioned at this point the wisdom of leaving the family farm. However he thought that:

Broadway is a very nice street but the rest of the town has the appearance of a business place. The people of New York dress exceedingly light and showy but they have a very unhealthy appearance and are very thin and spare of flesh.

This is an interesting observation, coming as it does from a farmer's son who must have spent a good deal of his time outdoors.

The following morning, 15 August, Young explored New York and decided to change some English money. For an unspecified number of Victorian pounds he appeared to get a rate per pound of four dollars and eighty-six cents, Very different to today!

On the same day Young went to the steamboat wharf where his luggage was weighed for his onward trip:

It weighed 70lbs. 50lbs is allowed free for each passenger. I had to pay 60 cents for extra weight to Buffalo, Therefore it is my experience carrying luggage about in any part of America. The company put a mass cheque (sic) *on plate on every package with the number on it and destination and they give you on e plate with a corresponding number on it. The plates are about the size of an English half Penny. The company are responsible for the luggage after it is properly chequed* (sic) *and transfer it from one car to another. At the end of your journey when you present your cheque the company have to produce your package with the corresponding number on the cheque attached to it and the destination. In default of which you have to value your luggage and the company pay you its value. If it is afterwards found you have to return the money and receive your luggage.*

All of this seems quite as complicated as travelling in the twenty-first century. William's onward journey beckoned.

ON THE ROAD AGAIN

WILLIAM YOUNG LEFT New York on the steamboat Erie at 6:00pm on 15 August. According to the *Erie Weekly Gazette* of 1837:

'The ERIE is of a beautiful model, and very substantially built. Her speed, it is said, will be 16 miles an hour. She will be finished by the opening of the Navigation, and is to be commanded by our townsman, Lieut. Ottinger of the cutter. Success attend the ERIE and her commander.'

Young had obviously made some connections, either in New York or perhaps on the voyage from England:

My friend J Little came to bid me good(bye) and the boat went off without giving any notice. We had to go to Pearmont and stop all night. It is 25 miles to Pearmont from New York. Arrived there at 8 pm and had to wait til 11 for the train during which time they removed the luggage from the steam boat to the cars by means of hand barrows two at one time. It is done at a rapid rate. No refreshments to be had except tea and coffee and that 6 cents per cup and nothing to eat with it.

Young's precise account of his expenditure comes in very useful in establishing costs in 1854, as well as revealing how basic long-distance travel in America often was at that time:

16th August. Travelling all night very slow. Stopped at every station. The name of the station is not called out as in England. The land is very hilly and the soil increasingly poor. The railway is made all along side of the river. There is no tunnelling the whole of the way. Very poor refreshments at all the stations. At 8.00pm arrived at Hoinsville station and had to part with my shipmates and no one that has not been to sea don't know how strong attachment grows in so short a time. Went opposite the station to sleep.

Open top wagons were sometimes used. William Young was now entirely on his own thousands of miles from home, having lost touch with the few friends he had made on the voyage.

City of Buffalo, a steel engraving from a study by A.C. Warren, engraved by W. Wellstood and published in 'Picturesque America', D. Appleton & Company, New York, New York 1873

On 17 August Young paid one quarter of a dollar for breakfast and caught the 9:00am express to Buffalo. With his farmer's eye he saw the quality of the land improving as he travelled:

Arrived there at 12 o'clock. Mr Sulley of the New England Hotel took my luggage and myself to his house at the corner of Michigan Street. Had very good accommodation at 7.5 cents per day and night. Walked about Buffalo all the afternoon and evening. Slept very well.

I travelled through Buffalo in the summer of 1975 as a young man on a Greyhound bus. It was not a pleasant experience and the passengers were advised not to leave the bus. It seems the risk of attack and robbery, at that time, was very real.

18th. Early had another walk nearly all over Buffalo. Met Mr McCulloch at the station. Buffalo is a much smaller looking place than New York. The houses at Buffalo are beautiful, animals slight and the ladies there are nice looking and dress remarkable neat.

This is quite different from the modern traveller's impression!

LAKE ERIE:
HOME FROM HOME

L AKE ERIE, NAMED after its indigenous Native American
people, is a banana-shaped lake with Detroit and Toledo at
its western end and Buffalo in the east. It is the most southerly of
the Great Lakes and is divided horizontally and roughly equally
between Canada and the United States. At the extreme eastern
end, Niagara Falls feeds water from Lake Erie into Lake Ontario.

The towns spread around its shores reflect the cosmopolitan
nature of its population. Port Dover in the north nearly opposite
Dunkirk to the south is an approximate copy of the position
of these towns in the English Channel. London and Middlesex
appear to the north of Port Dover while Norfolk is justifiably to
the east of London. There is even a River Thames! But Chatham
and Essex are to the west, as well as Cleveland, Hamburg and
Huron (named after the Native Americans), Sandusky and even
Mesopotamia. So it is nothing if not cosmopolitan. The lake
shore is dotted with small towns signifying plenty of industry, so
much so that Lake Erie became so extraordinarily polluted that
in 1952, the Cuyahoga river, discharging into the lake just west of
Cleveland on the southern shore, actually caught fire. A picture
shows flames from the lake engulfing a ship. The Clean Water Act
of 1972 solved some of these problems, but there are still sightings
of algae and E. coli outbreaks due to the occasional breakdown
of sewage systems. William Young eventually made his temporary
home on the north-eastern shore near Simcoe.

The Canadian province of Ontario borders Lake Erie to the north, with the US states of Pennsylvania and Ohio to the south, New York on the eastern shores and Michigan on the western side. Parts of the boundaries of the four states and Ontario lie within the lake. It is the fourth largest of the Great Lakes but also the shallowest; its depth ranges from only 19m to 64m at its deepest. The western basin is the most shallow. Erie is the smallest of the Great Lakes by volume of water but has a coastline of 1,286km. Water levels fluctuate with the seasons; the lowest level, surprisingly, is in the winter.

Landed at Port Dover at 8 am and was kindly received by English people. One asked us to stop at his house quite free of expense. The customs officers where (sic) very civil and wished us success in Canada. They did not examine my luggage. We left our luggage at the landing stage and walked to Mr Andrew Smith's, a relation of Mr McCulloch where treated in the best of manner. Indeed I consented to remain with them until I should get a situation.

Went to the Hookers at Port Ryersee Mills. Walked about there with Mr Hooker and Mr Hubbard. Slept there all night.

Young is now seriously in need of work.

21st. Received there three addresses from Mr H. Went over the mile and went back to Mr Smith's and slept all day.

On the 22 August, having spent a couple of days with contacts, Young calls at Windham Mill and took the stage to Walesford for $0.25.

Nearly engaged to live with Mr Park. Went over Mr Slack's new mill and stopped with him all night.

On 23rd William Young encounters some success in his search for work at the local mills.

Arose at 5 am and walked to Simcoe, a distance of 8 miles, before breakfast and engaged to work for Mr Wilton at Windham Mill for the first month at 18 dollars with board and lodging. Walked from there to Mr Adis and was received with the greatest kindness and had dinner with him and the workers.

Also on the 23rd, and despite his earlier walk, Young:

Walked to Port Ryersee and came through a large field of sand. No weeds or anything to be seen but hills of sand. Walked from Port Ryersee to Port Dover and paid 12 cents for a glass of ale. Only one I could get at that enormous price!

Reading William Young's diary nearly one hundred and seventy years later, I am left in admiration at the determination, fitness and adaptability of this youth in this strange New World and his ability to make friends and inspire confidence. He also gives the impression of wanting to make himself comfortable and feel at home as soon as possible. His succinct narrative style, albeit with a few misspellings, give a wonderful picture of mid-nineteenth century life on the American/Canadian border.

While Young's walks, up until now, may not seem exceptional in terms of distance, on 24 August he goes for what we might consider the jackpot.

On 18 August Young left Buffalo at 8:30pm on the steamboat *Plow Boy* and should have landed at Port Dover at 4:00am the following morning; he was delayed, however, by four hours due

Map of Lake Erie

to very dense fog on the lake.

Landed at Port Dover at 8 am and was kindly received by English people. One asked us to stop at his house quite free of expense. The customs officers where [*sic*] very civil and wished us success in Canada. They did not examine my luggage. We left our luggage at the landing stage and walked to Mr Andrew Smith's, a relation of Mr McCulloch where treated in the best of manner. Indeed I consented to remain with them until I should get a situation.

Went to the Hookers at Port Ryersee Mills. Walked about there with Mr Hooker and Mr Hubbard. Slept there all night.

21st. Received there three addresses from Mr H. Went over the mile and went back to Mr Smith's and slept all day.

On 22 August, having spent a couple of days with contacts, Young called at Windham Mill and took the stage to Walesford for $0.25:

Nearly engaged to live with Mr Park. Went over Mr Slack's new mill and stopped with him all night.

On 23 August William met with some success in his search for work at the local mills:

Arose at 5 am and walked to Simcoe, a distance of 8 miles, before breakfast and engaged to work for Mr Wilton at Windham Mill for the first month at 18 dollars with board and lodging. Walked from there to Mr Adis... and was received with the greatest kindness and had dinner [probably lunch!] with him and the workers.

On the same day, and despite his earlier walk, Young:

Walked to Port Ryersee and came through a large field of sand. No weeds or anything to be seen but hills of sand. Walked from Port Ryersee to Port Dover and paid 12 cents for a glass of ale. Only one I could get at that enormous price!

Reading the diary nearly 170 years later, I am left in admiration at the determination, fitness and adaptability of William Young in this strange New World, and his ability to make friends and inspire confidence. He also gives the impression of wanting to make himself comfortable and feel at home as soon as possible.

While Young's walks, up until now, may not seem exceptional in terms of distance, on 24 August he goes for what we might consider the jackpot:

Walked from the Smiths along the lake shore to Mrs Wells of South Cayuga, a distance of 33 miles and was very tired and thought of English ale, there being to be got to drink but whisky and spirits and water. The tavern keeper did not know what ale was. They were nearly all Dutch people. A great many could not talk English. The soil is very good there but gravelly timbered and the land is all sold and the fire were consuming acres and acres of good timber. And the soil as well as being very dry had no rain for 3 months and the weather very hot. No such thing as green, green grass to be seen and yet the cattle and houses are in good condition. I was received very kindly at the different places at where they understood me. Got at Mrs Wells at 7 pm.

William Young, it seems, had become just another immigrant in a nation made up of them.

On 25 August Young viewed the wreck of a steamer on Lake Erie that had come to grief a short time previously, and he saw several different species of large squirrel. The following day, after being pressured by Mrs Wells to stay longer, Young met the stage from Dunville to Dover. He commented on the locals' peculiar way of treating strangers when they enter a tavern but does not specify exactly what he means! Possibly there was a disconcerting silence. He arrived back at Mr Smith's at 2:00pm and had a good bath in Lake Erie as well as shooting some small birds in the afternoon. The summer was heading towards a close.

It is Sunday, 27 August:

Sunday reading [presumably religious] in the fornoon. Had an excellent dinner at Mrs Smith's and they rowed me down to Port Ryersee in the afternoon. Had tea at the Hookers and then walked to Mrs Adis and stopt [sic] all night.

On 28 August Young rode with Mr Adis to Simcoe early in the morning and started work at Windham Mill, chopping rye and preparing stones all day. He boarded and slept. On 29 August Young worked from 6:00am until 7:00pm, carrying out customer requirements and dressing small stones, a job he apparently enjoyed.

On August 30 Young bought some stationery:

Paid 1/5 for ½ quire paper and one packet envelopes [presumably to write home]. After stone dressing on 31 August, he made an interesting observation on 1 September: 'Saw some Indians but not quite in there [sic] native dress and thought I should like to go with them to spend a few years.

Perhaps Young, whose youth and foreign background rendered him relatively naïve, might have changed his mind had he known that, at this time, Native Americans in the fur-trapping regions north of the Great Lakes were still, in some cases, involved in scalping 'the white man' and, worse still, practising cannibalism! No doubt it was the exotic dress that attracted him although not all tribes, of course, adhered to these barbaric practices.

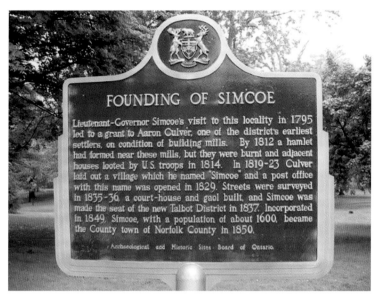

FOUNDING OF SIMCOE

Lieutenant-Governor Simcoe's visit to this locality in 1795 led to a grant to Aaron Culver, one of the district's earliest settlers, on condition of building mills. By 1812 a hamlet had formed near these mills, but they were burnt and adjacent houses looted by U.S. troops in 1814. In 1819-23 Culver laid out a village which he named "Simcoe" and a post office with this name was opened in 1829. Streets were surveyed in 1835-36, a court-house and gaol built, and Simcoe was made the seat of the new Talbot District in 1837. Incorporated in 1849, Simcoe, with a population of about 1600, became the County town of Norfolk County in 1850.

Archaeological and Historic Sites Board of Ontario

Simcoe: an introductory sign

LIEUT-COL. SAMUEL RYERSE
1752-1812

A United Empire Loyalist, Ryerse was commissioned in the 4th New Jersey Volunteers during the American Revolution, following which he took refuge in New Brunswick. In 1794 he came to Upper Canada, and the following year received 3,000 acres of land in Woodhouse and Charlotteville townships. Settling at the mouth of Young's Creek, he erected a grist-mill around which grew the community of Port Ryerse. As Lieutenant of the County of Norfolk and chairman of the Court of Quarter Sessions, he took an important part in the early military and civil administration of this area.

Erected by the Ontario Archaeological and Historic Sites Board.

Port Ryerse: an introductory sign

HARVEST TIME

THE YEAR HAD begun to wane and harvest time had arrived. William Young seemed to be being used for whatever work came to hand:

2nd September. Very busy taking in wheat all day. Took a walk through Simcoe in the evening. Did not like it quite so well.

At this time Simcoe was a very basic small town.

The next day, Sunday 3 September, Young took a walk for about two hours in the morning and then visited the English church and liked it very much:

Had a very good sermon and as usual their collection.

Using his recently acquired stationery Young spent the afternoon and evening at the Union Hotel writing home to Scotsford and the Kent village of Cowden, although we do not know what the latter meant to him.

4 September was very hot and Young complained about being thirsty all day. At 6:30pm he walked into Simcoe again. There was a full moon and this time Young found it very pleasant but complained that there was no library of any sort in the town. At that time Simcoe was a lakeside creation built mainly to service the local industry and without much in the way of culture. On 6 September he worked until 7pm, before heading to Simcoe yet again; he seemed to be suffering from homesickness:

Walked there until about 9 and came home thinking that England was the best place for comforts.

On 7 September Young started work at 5am, putting in what he describes as a hard day's work on various crops. Interestingly the prices he gives are in pounds sterling:

Wheat 6/- & corn 2/9, rye 3/-, bran 2/6 shoots 3/6, corn chop 8/- all in sterling.

September 8th. Packed 14lbs flour and then ground 60lbs of corn in 4 hours 5 minutes with 2 of 6 wide stones driven by an engine of the distillery. They run 350 times per minute.

9th. Rained all day. Rather cool. Packing flour and chipping.

10th. Sunday very poorly all night but got up at 7. Worked and went to River Lynn Mill in the afternoon. Mr Adis and myself went to Ryersee and had tea there and came home at 9 pm and went to bed.

11th. Packing flour and left off doing customer work.

12th. Sent off about 100 lbs of wheat. Chopping for distillery and went to apple tea and enjoyed myself very well at Mr Newell's.

13th. Sent off about 200 lbs of wheat and about 3000 lbs from Dover. Took a walk to River Lynn in the evening then began flouring for the first time that day.

14th. Not much to do all day. At J Dennis in the evening.

15th. Chopped 120 lbs corn in the distillery.

William Young seemed to be able to turn his hand to almost anything. Being physically able, he appeared to be fast becoming an invaluable member of the community. He came into contact with others from England, such as Mr Learey from Brighton. On 16 September, he was busy:

Stone dressing nearly all day. Went to Simcoe in the evening. White frost in the morning.

This seems surprising for September.

It seems Sunday was the only day of rest:

17th. Went for a work before breakfast and looked for the old mill. H Learey and myself went to Mr Adis in the morning. Stopped all day. Took a walk about the fields and woods [presumably to acclimatise himself to the area]. Hazel nuts quite ripe. We went to Mrs White's in the evening and had some peaches.

19th. Went to an Apple Bee in the evening. Good large party and enjoyed myself very well. Had the game of turn the wheel and others. Broke up at 2 o'clock.

20th. Cold morning. Chopping for the distillery and stone dressing. Sent off several loads of wheat to the lake.

21st. White frost and cold morning. Very warm in the day. Saw some ducks on Windham Pond. The appearance of Fall. So a first, hard Canadian winter was not far off.

22nd. Laid the chopping stones down and chopped 22 batches per hour for four hours and worked wheel drive about 300 times per minute.

23rd. Saw Mr Wilson. Told him about leaving and come to see Mr Adis in the evening. Mrs Adis poorly with the chill feaver.

24th. Sunday. H Learey and myself walked to Dover in the morning. Went to Smiths to dinner and came back to Simcoe at 8.

Although he does not say so, Young seemed to get on well with everyone he came in contact with, helping his chances to get work and making him popular. He appeared to be an industrious manual labourer:

25th. Nothing much to do in the mill. Went to Messrs Richie Ford. Gone to mill in the evening and spent 2 hours with Mr Walters' family. A resident of Lewes, he gave me two Lewes papers which was the first news I had of England since I left.

This connection with home must have been especially comforting. 26 September was William Young's last day at Windham Mill, before he went with Mr Pitcher to see Mr Wilson, who agreed to engage him at twenty-six dollars a month. After this:

Mrs Wilson spoke to me in rather milder tone. I came to River Lynn Mills in the evening. Agreed work with Mr Adis for 22 dollars.

Despite all the hard work, there were a few breaks for parties and suppers in what seems to be quite a close-knit community:

28th. Gusting all day and like it very much. 29th. Went to Mrs White's in the evening to an Apple Bee. Peeling peaches. Enjoyed it well. A different supper.

In an echo of the maypole dances in *The Wicker Man* (1973, d. Robin Hardy) it is interesting that parties were held around the harvesting of crops, with very little mention of any other food to accompany them. By October 1854, the days were getting colder and shorter.

1st. Sunday. At home nearly all day and wrote to William Hollands and enclosed a note to Mr Nicholson. Went to Mrs White's in the evening.

2nd. Went to Simcoe in the evening with Mr Adis. Saw Mr Wilson and had a plate of oysters.

4th. Went to Barryar and Simcoe.

6th. Went to Mrs White's in the evening to a Peach Bee.

Whilst a great deal of hard work was put in, there were also periods of well-deserved enjoyment, so Young did not seem to be in any way unhappy in his new environment. After all, there were apple bees, peach bees and oysters together with the accompanying socials to be enjoyed. On Sunday 8 September William was:

At home nearly all day. Took a walk in the evening. 10th. Very frosty mornings. Beautiful and clear sky. 12th. The commencement of Indian Summer which last about 14 days and is a very pleasant season.

The term 'Indian summer' was named after the Native Americans rather than the Indian sub-continent. On 18 October he:

Walked to Simcoe in the evening and saw Mr Wilson and received from him $18.

On 28 October Young received a letter from England containing news of his family, surely a welcome diversion. 29 October was wet, and Young spent all day at home as well as reading a paper that was sent from England.

By 4 November the weather had turned very cold with a little snow. Despite ice one and a half inches thick, Young was not put off and walked up the creek to see another waterfall. Curiously, at this point and most unlike Young's previously detailed account of his activities, the period covering 5–13 November is omitted. Perhaps Young was ill or perhaps he felt there was nothing worth reporting. What is clear is that the encroaching Canadian winter was going to be much harder than in William's native East Sussex.

On 14 November, Young received two Sussex newspapers from his mother, Oprah. On 19 November Young lunched at Mr White's in Simcoe and had tea at Mr Noel's before walking home on what he refers to as a dark and presumably cold night. On November there was a:

Snow storm, cold weather a little sleighing. 22nd. Finished flouring for this Fall and very glad of it. 23rd. Frosty weather. Pond all frozen over.

The weather remained like this for nearly a week until:

24th. Weather changed very rapid. Snow all gone but very dirty on the roads.

This enabled Young to plant winter cabbages the following day. He was nothing if not adaptable. The following Sunday (26 November):

Harry and myself walk to Harry Hubbard's at Ryersee and met the Dover boys there. Spent the day very comfortable. All English and quite a snug party.

Unfortunately the snow came on again in the afternoon and Richard White brought them home at 10:00pm.
On 27 November Young reports:

Hog killing. Killed 5 or rather murdered them.

This is rather a surprising comment, perhaps an example of black humour. A day later, William:

Helped Mr Adis cut up the hogs in the morning. Gusting came along about 11 and we continued busy all day. Frosty weather and cold.

By December 1854 it was mid-winter:

3rd. Deep snow. Went for a sleigh ride in the morning. Came home and stayed in all day. Went to bed early.

4th. Rose at ½ past 1 and went stone dressing. Very cold. In the evening went to Simcoe in the cutter and was nearly frozen. Had the cramps in the night as a consequence.

The following day Young received a newspaper from Mrs Banfoot and paid $2 for a subscription to *The New York Tribune* for the year commencing 1 January 1855, confirming his intention to stay around for a while. Little did he know, however, that the markers were slowly beginning to be put in place for the forthcoming American Civil War.

What with the deep winter starting to bite and Young's apparent enjoyment of sleighing, it is unsurprising that he decides to invest in some warmer clothing:

Paid $4 for gloves and cap. About this time wrote to Mr Holland. Paid Mrs White 15/- for three pairs of socks... Paid $6.50 for a pair of long boots at Mrs Murphey.'

Given that this was 1854, the boots seem fairly expensive. As luck would have it, he had no sooner bought them than on 11 December than the snow began to thaw and the weather turned much less cold. The next day, however, Young suffered from tooth ache nearly all night, but we are not told how he dealt with this. Instead on 13 December he went to Simcoe and paid $4.50 for another pair of boots and $3 for two flannel shirts. He also ate a plate of oysters. Young's bank balance was partly restored by receiving $20 from Mr Adis as wages due. By 16 December, William reports:

Snow nearly all gone. Warm weather and very dirty.'

The 17th December raises the spectre of Prohibition:

We all went round to the school house and Dr Crouse and others lecture on temperance. The doctor was drunk at the time [!] but talk pretty sensible. There was a great majority in favour of a prohibitory law - a good attendance of hearers. The first time I walked with a girl arm in arm since I left England.

Sadly, we are not told who the girl was! In such a harsh environment, especially in the winter, it is good to know that William Young appeared to have been so quickly absorbed into the community.

By 18 December the snow had returned with a vengeance and Young spent a very dull day at home with nobody around. The following day it was very cold and frosty and the wheel gate froze up continuously. Young has another touch of homesickness:

Began to think England was better than Canada.

By 20 December, he reports:

Cold clear, no wind. Cleaning the smut room out.

The next day he works near the pond, cutting down wood.

At this point, close to Christmas, Young expressed his doubts about religion. On 22 December Young was still very busy and the weather turned slightly warmer. He again suffered from tooth ache but despite this, worked through part of the night. There was still much work in the night and pretty good sleighing. On 23 December he listed the prices of all the crops and subsidiaries, e.g. buckwheat six shillings, corn seven shillings and oats four and sixpence. Only a few items, like flour, are expressed in dollars, either Canadian or American.

On 24 December disaster suddenly struck:

Simcoe Mills and distillery burnt down. Belonging to Riche, Ford & Jones. 12,000 bails of wheat destroyed, other corn and flour and a good quantity of whiskey. Warm weather. Mr H Learey came in the morning. At home all morning and all went to the fire in the afternoon.

However, it is not stated whether arson was the cause, as it often had been in this area, and the fire did not apparently prevent

William Young from enjoying a Christmas Eve party with singing and two roast geese:

Alack Colman and the Miss Woolnough here in the evening. The Miss White and others. We had singing and a comfortable party.

The formal way that Young addresses the ladies in his diary demonstrates his respect for them, something we seem to have lost in the twenty-first century.

Here is Young's account of Christmas Day, 1854:

Warm weather. Very dirty. Went shooting in the forenoon with N L, H L and Richard Fry. Kill some black squirrels and a few little birds. I killed an owl with a rifle [The slaughter of birds in the diary seems quite indiscriminate]. In the afternoon I went to the silver mine and tried there mineral balls to ascertain the veins of silver. Came home and went to play cribbage and went to bed at 11 after spending a very good Xmas in Canada. Had some elderberry wine, 2 geese, 1 turkey and plum pudding.

Amazingly after all that festivity, Young was up at 2:00am the next day, 26 December, and grinding thirty-five bails of wheat. This was completed by 5:30am before he went rifle-shooting. Then, after another three hours' work in the mill, he went shooting again with Harry Learey and R. Fry. The unfortunate victims were a black squirrel and an owl. Compare this work ethic with our own, over our much-extended Christmas!

The following day he was at work in the mill but being dogged by toothache again, especially at night. 28 December was a very wet day with little work, so William decided it was time to get to grips with the toothache:

I went to Dr Salmon at Simcoe. Had 3 teeth taken out... I took a common dose of chloroform but with no effect. I tried a double dose but still with little effect except for a rapid beating of the heart & loss of sight. I could hear the clock tick and was conscious of their feeling my pulse. I fancied I heard a rumply sound for a little while but quite recovered from the effects of it before they began [to] operate on my teeth. Charge a half $ per tooth. Felt a pain over my eyes all the evening and went to bed early.

Despite this horrific and, by modern standards, brutal surgery, Young reports that on:

'29th. Felt very comfortable with regard to tooth ache. Frosty weather and rather cold. Busy in the mill.'

The following day he was:

'Posh stone dressing. In the evening very sleepy.'

This is not surprising after all the dental work! On New Year's Eve he:

'Went to meeting in the morning. At home all afternoon alone. Wrote to Scotsford.'

And so ended what must have been a momentous year for William Young, without apparently any sort of New Year gathering.

1855: A BUSY YEAR

DESPITE THE FACT that it was New Year's day, William Young was up at 3:00am:

> *1st. Stone dressing. Very little gusting. With H Learey. Almost a general holiday. Clear. Party.*

He was similarly active on 2 January and remarks on the beautiful weather:

> *3rd. Warm weather. I went to Simcoe to More's Hotel at the freemen's dinner. Paid $1 for ticket. Music, drink and everything included. First rate dinner. Turkey and roast pigs. Good music and singing. Enjoyed myself well. Happy party... Broke up at 12. I went and slept at H Learey's.*

One of the most remarkable things about William Young is his willingness and ability to adapt to a variety of different jobs, start incredibly early in the morning and work hard and efficiently. This must have made him an invaluable member of the local community. He seemed to possess a remarkable energy as well as being extremely precise in his accounting for work done and money spent:

> *January 5th. Flouring for Mrs Schylen at 3 yd/yankee dollars/per batch.*

Young goes into more calculations and on 6 January he visits Wisconsin & the miller's house in Illinois.

On Sunday 7 January he entertained at home:

Gilbert and Mr Nelson came from Waterford. Miss White here.

Although there is no comment to that effect, William Young might well have had his eye on Miss White! There are some things, it seems, perhaps too personal even for a diary!

On 9 January, he reports being very busy in the mill gusting all day and reading in the evening. He also reports that he:

Went after Eliza in the evening and the night before at the White's.

On 10 January:

Went to the other mill and look over that. Not very busy. After reading Bill's letter from England I thought I should like to go home. Highly pleased with the letter.

In the depths of a Canadian winter and after six months abroad, Young was, unsurprisingly, homesick.

On 11 January:

Snow fell in the night. Rather dull day. Thought of England. 12th. This is the January gales. Plenty of water.

The following day the temperature fell from 37 to 25°C in five hours. There seem to have been some large variations in temperature over the mid-winter period. Nevertheless Young carried on with the stone dressing. On Sunday 14 January he spent the whole day at home:

Harry Learey, Miss White and Mr and Mrs Adis went to Ryersee.

On 15 January he:

Went to Simcoe in the evening and to Willson's Mills. Paid $1 for different articles. Walked home rather tired.'

The following day there was:

A little snow. All went out in the woods but me. Sold 1700 flour, 200 buck wheatflour chop. Money taken $72.25.

He also bought, inter alia, some wheat. There is a long list of goods bought and sold. Because of Young's attention to detail, he seems to have been a pretty sharp operator, administratively as well as practically.

Busy day. Miss Tivetale here. Mrs Adis poorly. Finished reading The Hall & the Cottage by Mrs Ellis. A very good tale in the Guide to Social Happiness by Mrs Ellis. This appears to be one of the self-improvement manuals that were very popular at the time.

On 17 and 18 January Young was up early and working hard all day. On 19 January there was:

Not much gusting along. I went to Simcoe in the evening for sawing 1,000 feet of fret board measure pine.

A detailed account then follows of what this involved:

Received $4 from Mr Adis in part of wages. Good ride.

20 January was another busy day. Young notes being short of water. He carried on stone dressing into the evening and went to bed early, exhausted. As the following day, Sunday, was snowy, he stayed at home all day and wrote to his Uncle Mansen and J. Dodd in Liverpool. He then went to bed early.

On 22 January Young:

Rose at 3 o'clock rather reluctantly and went stone dressing. Cold, sleepy, and very stormy. Thought of England. Hardly any gusting. All day continued snow storm.

In the depths of a bleak Canadian winter this is scarcely surprising. English winters can be demanding but they do not usually come close to this in severity. This hardship may also explain why William Young worked so assiduously. However, he also enjoyed some sport:

23rd. Good sleighing. Up early, slept with Mr Adis. Gusting came fast. Very busy with 47 saw logs. Canada [is] the place for business but very cold at work. And tired. 24th. First rate sleighing and 60 logs came in.

The following day:

'Peter Bennett went away. J Culver came here. I rose at 4 o'clock and went to Dover.'

On 26 January:

Great trouble with the wheel gate. Continuously froze. Saw logs come in fast. Cold weather.

At that time there was a great deal of bartering of goods and services; by Sunday 28 January Young was looking for a change:

J. Culver, Eliza Berghaus and I went to Staleford Meeting House. Elder Hack preached a pretty good sermon. Spent the day at Mrs Berghaus. Very pleasantly slated house. Spent all day at Mrs Berghaus very pleasantly. Started home at 6 o'clock. Upset the cutter. Threw us all out. Got off without injury. A good rolling in the snow. Came as far as Simcoe and slept at the Baptist Chapel. Got home at 9.

29th. Very windy. Continued snowing all day. No gusting. Shot 3 geese in the morning. Went shooting with J Culver in the afternoon.

30th. Still very blusterous and snowy. Very little stirring.

By 31 January the weather had become much pleasanter but another problem arose:

Had a pain in my side all day. Went to bed early. 1st February. My side rather worse... 2nd. Still rather poorly. Did not do much work all day.

By 3 February Young had decided it was time to take some action as the problem was interfering with his work:

Got up hastily. Mr Adis in the cog pit. Pleasant but cold weather. I went to Simcoe in the morning. Saw Dr Salmon and got a plaster and a pot of pills. Pills 2 yd. Plaster 3 yd.

Young even tells us the price! Nothing seemed to put off his precise recording of all transactions, even when he was unwell. Fortunately these medicines seem to have had an effect:

4th. Sunday. Mr and Mrs Adis went to Ryersee. Harry and the Dover Boys came in the afternoon. Miss White here. My side much better. Harry slept with me.

5th. Harry agreed with Mr Adis. Very clear and pleasant weather but remarkably cold. Sun shone out bright. The coldest day of the winter so far. Harry came in the evening. Wheel gate continuously froze up. Sweet Canada!

But worse was to come:

6th. H Learey at work here. The coldest day that has been for years, 10 below zero. Mr Adis froze his face. Rather busy day. Wheel froze. 2 hours before we could start. The thermometer stood at 27 degrees below zero out of doors.

7th. 3 hours before we could start the wheel. Cut a good deal of ice from the wheel. Too cold to be comfortable. 8 below.

However, there was an improvement on 8 February. It was not quite so cold and Young received two letters, one from Frank and one from Scotsford Farm. He was obviously keeping in touch with his family who must surely have been worried about him. Although he took out a subscription to *The New York Tribune* more than two months previously, the first copy only arrived on 9 February.

On the same evening William, Miss White (about whom he still seems quite coy!) and Eliza Berghaus went to Dover for a:

...tea meeting for 3 yd per ticket. Had $2 in change from Mr Adis. Had a good supper and enjoy myself very well. A great number of laydes [sic]. They all went in the cutter and got home at half past twelve.

On 10 February Young reported a hard week's work with breakfast at 6:00am before working through until midnight. So by Sunday 11 February it is not surprising that he reports being:

Rather poorly. Stay'd at home all day. Snow storm.

By Monday he was better:

12th. Went to work in earnest. Left off at 10. 13th. Sent a paper to Scotsford. A rather wet day. Machine to thaw and not so busy as usual.

Young then provides us with a list of current prices for crops such as $3.25 for corn meal and $2 for wheat. On 14 February he was:

Up in the night. Drew some water. Cut the ice from the wheel. Snow going fast. 15th. Up stone dressing. Dressed a stone close in 6 hours and ground 109 buck wheat in 11 hours. Busy day.

It was 16 February and Young was very tired in the evening. So, time for some relaxation!

17th. Up early. Work hard all day. Left off work at 11 pm and went up to Whites after Eliza came home at 1 o'clock.

18th. Sunday. Went for a sleigh ride in the morning to the beech woods and in the evening we all went to Simcoe to church. A subscription in aid of the widows and orphans of the British and French soldiers. I gave 6 yd. Beautiful and pleasant reading.

But on 19 February William was:

Up at work at 3 am and very busy all day. Flour for Mr Keller.

The next few days were very busy as winter began to relent. This made working conditions easier:

20th. Very busy day. Beautiful and clear weather.

21st. Not quite so busy. Sleighing and so good.

Young made the best of any enforced downtime:

22nd. Most of the ice off the wheel [gone]. Gusting average 100lbs per day and chopping about as much. Sent a paper to Mr Hollis.

23rd. Cold day. Severall [sic] ducks round about. Went down to the beech woods in the evening. Rough road.

24th. Went for a walk in the morning and saw a deer track. Went up to the Whites and got in company with a person from Cornwall in England and travelled to different parts. Some time at the Brazils. Interesting talk.

25th. Sunday. Wrote to Fanny. A very clear and cold day. At home most of the time.

26th. Rather busy. Had some talk with a man that has been over from Ireland and other parts... Made 8,043 lbs of flour.

The picture of William Young that is emerging is that, despite all the hard and lengthy work, he had an enquiring mind, attending lectures on such subjects as anatomy even before leaving England. The subscription to *The New York Tribune* suggests he was a young man who was keen to educate himself.

But winter had not finished with that part of Canada yet!

27th. Very cold. Wheel froze. O the joys of Canada winter!

By 28 February the ice was sixteen inches thick:

Harry and O'Byers getting ice for the summer. Sent a letter to Fanny and one enclosed to Bill H. March. 1st. Paid Mrs Murphy $2.50 for Lorenzo Life and journal on the dealings of God, Man and the Devil.

Young never stopped reading, whether it was news, self-help or quasi-religious tracts.

3rd. Mr Watson here. Put some buckets in the water wheel. Rather milder weather. Snow inclined to rain. Miss Maus here for the evening. 4th. Pleasant morning. Mr and Mrs Adis went to Fort Rowan. At home all day. Miss White here.

By 5 March a thaw had set in with a little rain:

Saw mill commenced to run. Mr and Mrs Adis came home.

The following day Young reports a beautiful and warm day and a great deal of water, presumably from the sudden thaw.

7th. Commenced flouring for ourselves. Not a great deal of gusting. In the evening Mr and Mrs Adis and myself went to Mrs Hooker's. Mr Adis and me went to a dinner party at Port Ryersee. We paid $2 per ticket in aid of the Paternotre Fund. Not a very good attendance. Coming home I upset the cutter but did not hurt us. Got home at 6pm. Received a paper from Mrs Burfoot, one from Frank and one from Oprah. One letter from Frank and Oprah enclosed and one from Fanny and Oprah and father enclosed. All today. All somewhat cool but Frank's and that was lively and cheering.

The cold and windy weather soon returned but Young hardly noticed as he was hard at work again with stone dressing, until midnight on 9 March.

10th. Up early and finished my stones. 6 and a half hours at one stone... 12am. Rather sleepy.

11th. Harry and I went to Dover. From there we walked to Mrs Smith's. Walked a long distance and on the lake a rather rugged bird. Very thick and strong. Went to race course on the lake. 8 horses ran last week. Cold day. William Lean came home with us. Dark in the evening with some more snow.

12th. Not quite so busy. Saw mill cutting some beautiful black walnut. Papered the office with old county papers.

But by 13 March winter had returned:

13th. Cold. Rained and froze as it fell. At noon commenced to snow. Continued to snow all day. Good sleighing again.

14th. About eight inches of snow and good sleighing. A very busy day at work. At work all night at gusting. Had 320 bails of gusting of all sorts. Rained in the night and the snow went off. A great deal of water.

15th. Wheel flooded. Left off work at 6 am.

On 16 March things had improved:

Pleasant weather. Busy day at work. Now 12 o'clock. Sleepy. Kept work till 2 pm. Jane Marr here.

17th. Beautiful weather. Clear and frosty. At work late.

A break in the routine was well overdue.

A TRIP TO NIAGARA

18th. Sunday. Walked to Dover with Mr Learey. Very dirty – bad walking. Slept at J Innes Tavern Farmers' Inn. First rate bed.

19th. Got up at 6 o'clock. Went to J Smith's. Half past 8 took the stage from Dover to Caledonia. 32 miles. Paid $1.25. Got to Caledonia at 12. Paid 3 yd for dinner at Caledonia. Took the stage to Hamilton where I walked about the town. Saw one of my ship mates. Slept at Miles Tavern, King Street. Comfortable and respectful house.

20th. Paid 7 yd for supper, bed and breakfast. Paid 1 yd for cleaning my boots. Had a good ramble about Hamilton in the morning.

After these outgoings – and it is not clear why Young went on this journey – he obviously felt in need of a change. Perhaps it was a well-earned break. He adds as an afterthought at the bottom of the page that he had received $25 as part of wages due which would have helped fund the trip.

March 20th. 11am. Took the Great Western Railway to the Suspention [sic] Bridge. Got there at 1 pm. Got rid of our yankee companions.

He sounds rather pleased about that. We don't know if his attitude was political or personal but we have all experienced unwelcome fellow travellers.

Niagara Falls daguerreotype – an early form of photograph (c.1840)

Paid 10/1 yd fare. Walked to the falls on the Canada side and slept there all the afternoon. Went over the museum and Indian sanctuary and saw the buffalos. Skeleton of a whale. Splendid flowers in the hothouses. Cut a cedar stick close to the falls, and entered my name in the register under the Laneys (both of Port Dover) on the 20th March 1855. The ice looks beautiful at the falls. Cold day. Slept at Mr Pike's Elgin Hotel close to the suspention [sic] bridge.

The suspension bridge was new at the time of Young's visit. Niagara's name derives from the Mohawk Indians and consists of three falls at the southern end of Niagara Gorge, originally formed by receding glaciers. The largest is the Horseshoe Falls (57m high) which forms the boundary line between Canada and the USA. The Bridal Veil Falls and the American Falls are both in the United States. Young was at the far eastern end of Lake Erie, where the Niagara River drains into Lake Ontario. With the largest flow rate of any waterfall in North America and a drop of more than 50m, Niagara must have been an incredible sight for William Young, who would have been more accustomed to the gentle East Sussex countryside. This daguerreotype, by the English industrial chemist Hugh Lee Pattinson, is the earliest known picture of the Falls.

Another Englishman, Captain Matthew Webb, drowned trying to swim the rapids, downriver from the Falls, in 1883. In 1875 he had become the first man to swim the English Channel.

21st. Walked over the suspention [sic] bridge. Had a thorough look at that. Paid 2 yd to go over. Went to the town of Niagara and saw the falls yankee side. The Falls and the Suspension bridge are the two most stupendous works of nature and art I ever saw. The span of the suspension bridge 820ft 4,860 wires in each great cable, 4 in number. Ampira, a French philosopher, estimates the cataract of Niagara at 4,533,144 horsepower or nineteen times all the motive power of Great Britain [or Brunel's ship?] or more than sufficient to drive all the factories in the world. Paid 9 yd for a bad bed. Slept in Hamilton and had dinner. 3 yd. Took train from there to Paris. 7 yd. Went through Paris to Stage to Brantford and from there to Simcoe. 32 miles fare 10 yd all the way. Cold ride. Got to Simcoe about 2 at night and slept at Mr Boughness comfortably. Paid 3 yd for bed and breakfast. Took the train from the suspension bridge to Hamilton by express. 10 yd fare.

Young's detailed observations show that he might well, with training, have made a good engineer.

Niagara Falls c.1850 (artist unknown)

Niagara Falls Suspension Bridge 1855 (artist unknown)

AN ERIE SPRING

March 22nd. Went up to Windham Mills in the morning and then went to the court house and heard a good trial about Dr Bowey not setting Mr Smit's leg well after it was broken. £130 in damages, verdial fin fracture. Interesting. Came home about 8:00pm and spent in all my ramble $19 and enjoyed myself well.

23rd. Not much gusting. Snowed all day. Stone dressing - did it well.

24th. Good sleighing. Good deal of gusting. Stone dressing. In the evening chopping run. Mrs Adis. Paid $22 for a new saw.

Given the extraordinarily early hour at which Young sometimes started work, it is a sobering thought that he only seemed to get Sundays off. Even then he was quite busy:

25th. Sunday. Richard Fry here. H. Hubbard. All went down to the other mill in the afternoon. Began to write to Frank. 26th. A regular snowstorm. Stone dressing.

But then the worst happened:

27th. First symptoms of chill fever. Very poorly all night. Mr Keys' flum broke away. Obliged to clear the water down. Sick all day. Did not work. Restless night.

28th. Little better. About in the mills nearly all day. Cold day.

29th. Very bad cough and rather busy.

Given that it was now the end of March, I think the diary gives a clear idea of the harshness of the Canadian climate: it was still snowing and bitterly cold:

31st. Very pleasant day. Great deal of snow. Went away. In shade 7 degrees.

April 1st. Sunday. Cold and windy. At home all day. Great trouble in getting two pieces of trees from under the gates. Cough rather bad.

2nd. A letter to Frank and enclosed a note to Oprah.

3rd. Much pleasanter. Sleepless night. Bad cough.

4th & 5th. Very poorly with my cough and cold. Two wild turkeys settled here. Could not get them.

6th. Good Friday. Had two millwrights at work at the new mill. Several past along. Nothing at all the appearance of a holiday.

After what seemed an endless winter Young reports that

April 7th. Snow gradually disappearing. Frosty mornings but pleasant days. A little appearance of Spring but no birds singing. Went to Simcoe in the evening.

8th. Sunday. At home all day. Jane Marr here and rather poorly.

9th. Not much gusting. Dug the flower garden up. Shot some birds.

10th. Ice all gone from the water wheel. Very muddy roads.'

There follows a detailed account of current crop prices and the cost of sending them to New York.

On 11 April William 'Sent a letter to Mr Lancelay, Montreal P. O.' but he does not say why. Sometimes we are left with tantalising glimpses of other lives that are not developed in the diary.

12th. Wrote a letter to Frank and sent it off. A little note to Mrs H. Rather busy. Roads begin to dry up. Gardening a little.

13th. Beautiful day. At work in the sawmill in the morning.

14th. Fallowed up the garden. Warm day. Much gusting.

15th. The pleasantest Sunday for some time. Up early. Walk up the side of the lake. Some ducks and two wild geese. Saw several handsome birds. Went with Doris and a friend to the Catholic church at Simcoe. Liked it well. Came home by Owen's saw mill. Site for sale. 15 feet fall. Price $5000. Weather just warm enough. Got home at 2 o'clock. Stopped at home till 5. Then went home with Jonnee Main. Nice girl, apprentice of Werrett. At home reading Columbus voyage and travels. Finished reading Lorenzo Dous.

16th. Busy day... Lizards and frogs make a great noise and handsome birds make their appearance.

On 17 April Young reports a heavy thunder storm with much lightning. Apparently:

Very busy all day... Did all the work myself. The fish bite well all day! 18th. General fast stops both mills. Had about 100lbs of gusting. I went for a ride with Mr Adis in the pine woods. Found some winter berries and kill one snake.

Despite the recent snow Young reports that it was a very hot day. He seems to have got his dates muddled because there are two different reports for 18 April:

Maple sap ran well. Drank some. (Canada is of course a primary source for maple syrup.) *Made a raft in the morning and went on the creek. A snap turtle on the lake here weighed about 38lbs. A very heavy thunder storm in the night and rain.*

It is surprising how quickly the weather went from very wintry at the beginning of April to something like summer:

19th. A large flock of geese here. Hot day. Very busy.

20th. Wet morning. Nothing much today. Stone dressing in the evening. Shot 2 English snipes. Idle day. Received a paper from Frank.

21st. Beautiful day. Wheat and grass growing very fast.

22nd. Went up the creek in the morning and then at home all day. Mr L and Richard Fry rather apprentice Mr Adis in the morning.

23rd. Caught several fish with my hands. Rose wheat to 14 yd, corn $1, flour $4.75. Received a paper from F. Manser.

Young seemed to enjoy shooting and fishing between extended bouts of hard work:

24th. Shot a duck in the morning. Commenced getting up at 5 o'clock. Bought a new gun off Mr Walker for $20. Received $20 in part of wages. 25th. Wheat 15 yd. Sent a paper to England. Rather wet day.

26th. Sent a paper to Father marked with 4 months before I go home.

This clearly indicates that it was supposed to be a temporary posting, perhaps to gain experience.

Finished flouring in the afternoon. Caught some fish.

27th. Frosty morning. Shot some birds. Snow banks all gone.

28th. Navigation open as far as Erie but not to Buffalo.

29th. At home reading in the morning & walked to Ryersee in the afternoon. Went in a boat on the lake. Saw thousands of ducks and a good quantity of geese. Went to H Hubbard's for tea... Got home at 8:00pm.

Perhaps because of the harsh winter, crop prices were now extremely high:

Flour rose to $5, the highest this has been in this part of Canada and wheat to $2. Went shooting in the afternoon. Saw some quails and a bald eagle. Potatoes 5 yd.

May 1st. Beautiful morning but no garlands of flowers. England much pleasanter at this time of the year. Mr Adis sick with the chill fever and ague [feverish and shivering].

2nd. Received a Sussex paper from Frank.

3rd. Mr and Mrs Adis went to Brandford. Rather wet morning. About the midst of oat sowing now. Birds begin to build their nests.

4th. Very busy day. Earned $12 after dinner with one run of stones.

5th. Went shooting in the morning. Beautiful and clear. Sent a paper to Frank. Thought I should like to continue in Canada.

6th. At home in the morning. In the afternoon went to Mr Steinhoff's and then to Simcoe and looked over Riches' new mill and the ruins of the old one.

Sadly, despite it being early May, winter returned with a vengeance:

7th. Dark dismal cold day with a snowstorm in the afternoon. Price of lumber at Ryersee cleared very good $18 4c... cash at Dover about $1 per 1,000 more. 8th. Snowing all night. Ground covered. Very unusually cold and wet. Wheat at $2 per bale, flour $5.25 per 100. Sale of goods leaving a profit with ready money and plenty of sale.

9th. Left off snowing. Very busy gusting. 10th. Received a paper from Oprah. Beautiful fine day. 11th. Earned $24 in the mill gusting. Sent a paper to Frank.

After another wet day on 12 May, the following day Young took a walk on a very rough road from Dover to where the wreck of the *Favourite* lay:

Went in a boat to the wreck and got on board. Rode home with Mr Bowers. Humming birds came.

There are perhaps 2,000 shipwrecks on Lake Erie alone (Laura Johnson, 2017), and on the other Great Lakes, many thousands of lives were lost in over 20,000 wrecks. This might seem odd for inland waterways. However, the sheer scale of the lakes – Erie alone being 241 miles long and 57 miles wide – along with shallows and sudden storms, have created an extraordinary number of wrecks. About 375 have been found so far in Erie alone. Combined with

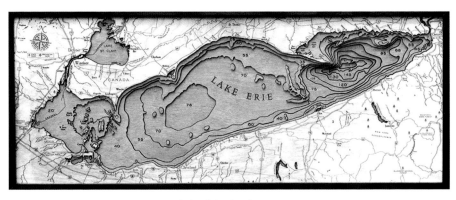

Lake Erie depth map

the harsh climate and lack of natural harbours, the Great Lakes are therefore not friendly for navigation.

The next day, 14 May, the navigation finally opened to Buffalo. Perhaps this really was the end of winter:

First trip of the Plowboy. Stone dressing in the evening.

On 15 May, William reports being:

Busy and rather short of water' and, on 16 May, *Received $34 as part of wages. Went to Dover.*

From this point on William's diary entries become less regular and do not necessarily follow on logically:

June 21st. Up and did a little stone dressing before breakfast. Feel rather tender. 3 papers came during my absence: one from Frank, one from Spencer and one from Fanny and Oprah. Wheat out in ear and clover in full blossom.

24th. Sunday. At home all day. One letter to Oprah, father & family. Rather wet. Went out in boat.

25th. Up at half past four stone dressing. Flowers all out in blossom. Some wild strawberries ripe. Time to sow buck wheat.

Young then provides some crop prices with that precise eye of his. Also on 25 May, he:

Went out in boat in the evening. Mostly moon high. Very pleasant.

26th. Had a little turn flouring. Made above 150lbs. 28th. Not much gusting. Rather too warm to be pleasant.

The following few days Young was hard at work but with time for reflection:

29th. Just 12 months ago I left home. Hot. Thunder storm. In the sun went up to Simcoe after supper and then Harry, Mr Adis and me went to Dover. Came back. Harry, Miss White, Charlotte and me went out in the boat for a while on the pond. One o'clock in the morning. Moonlight and very pleasant.

30th. Richard came home. Not much gusting. Loading logs and lumbering all day. Shooting with the rifle and on the creek with the boat in the evening.

Another month turns:

July 1st. Sunday. Went down the creek as far as we could go in the boat and a smart job to get it back in the afternoon. CA, MJ, L, HL, and me went strawberrying... Out on the pond in the evening.

2nd. Not much to do. Commenced to furrow the Chappa presumably a customer] run of stone.

3rd. Mr & Mrs Adis went to Brantford. I took sick. Came back. Laying about now. Begin to change to cooler pleasant weather.

4th. Slack time in the mill and expect to prepare for Fall work. Sick with the dull fever. Very prevalent now.

5th. Sent a paper to Mrs Burford. Received $10 from Mrs Adis in part of wages. Paid 5 yd for a pound of gun powder and ½ yd for 200 caps. 6th. Had the first ripe cherries this year from Mrs White. Furrowing the stones days when I get time.

7th. Flour $5. Wheat $2. Practising rifle shooting in the evening. 100 loads for my rifle cost $0.5 including caps and powder.

8th. Sunday. Received a letter from Fanny. Wrote to Mr C Wells in the morning and went up to Mrs White's and Miss Austin in the afternoon. Had plenty of cherries. Quite a party of us out in the boat in the evening. Alexandrina Woolnough! Worked to half past one. 6 o'clock of Sunday.

Over a year since he left home in Hartfield, William Young worked hard over the following days:

July 9th. Busy gusting. Up at 2 o'clock and finished flouring.

10th. Not over hot. Most always a good breeze.

11th. Busy gusting.

12th. Stone dressing in the morning. On the pond in the evening.

13th Letting in the bow of the down stream run of stones. Quite a job to cut out the lead. Pretty good day's work!

UNDER THE WEATHER

WILLIAM YOUNG'S FINAL days in Canada were blighted with bad luck:

14th. Rather sick.

15th. Sunday. We all three walked to Dover. Stop at S Innes. Had some green peas for dinner. Plenty about now.

17th. Got a piece of steel in my eye. Bad all night. Not any sleep.

Workers at that time, of course, usually had little in the way of protection.

18th. My eye very bad. Had on a poltice [sic] of slippery elm to draw it. Got better towards morning. Alum curd good to help the inflammation from the eye. Put a quantity of powdered alum in new milk, stir it till it curdles. Then had it on a new cloth and paste it on the eye.

William Young often mentions a paper he has read or been given. I believe this refers to something less formal than the current sense of the word 'paper', especially where his family were concerned. They were probably more like the 'round robin' letters some families send out at Christmas and, as often as not, bore the pants off anyone who is not a close family member.

19th. Received a paper from Oprah and a piece of paper with love on it marked with Fanny's name and address. Weather very hot. Too hot to be pleasant. Flies and mosquitoes about very much. Thermometer stood at 90 degrees in the sun and at 92 degrees in the shade. [Surely the other way round?] A violent storm came after dinner and a great whirlwind. Thundered and rain all the afternoon.

20th. Not quite as hot. Commenced to cradle wheat.

21st. My eye rather bad and very busy gusting. Showery weather.

22nd. Went across the pond in the morning and got some wild gooseberries and raspberries. Quite ripe and good. In the afternoon all went to Mrs White's and had a blow out of cherries there. Out on the pond.

23rd. Ate too many cherries. Sick all night and poorly all the next day. Wet.

The concentration on one item of fruit is, of course, likely to have had that result in all but the most hardened of stomachs!

24th. Regular wet day. Very unusual at this time of year. Bad harvesting.

25th. Cloudy, rather dull English weather. Quiet afternoon. Warmer. Up at Simcoe at a circus. Very good one. Rain in torrents most of the way home. Got home at 12.

26th. Still wet. Wheat growing and quite ripe.

27th. Stone dressing and furrowing. Then out. Left off raining in the afternoon.

28th. Rotary gusting, furrowing the stones and hot.

29th. Walked to Lois Lewis' steam saw mill in Windham centre. Called and saw several of my favourite customers. Had dinner at Mr Duncan Green's. Saw Henry Bennett the first time. Walk home in the evening by the railway track. Wind and lightning and dark. Bad walking; mosquitoes troubled me. Call at the Bughners and stay a little while. Cleaned up there then started for home. Rather tired. Walked home thirty miles in all and hot [an amazingly long trek on foot].

Then William Young had more bad luck:

30th. Still showery. Got another piece of steel in my eye. Very painful all night.

August 1st. Eye bad and showery again. Gust mill flume broke down. In the evening went to Ryersee with Mrs Adis. My eye still bad.

2nd. Cannot see to dress stone. Mrs Bowen here for the flour.

3rd. All day my eye bad. Did not do much work.

4th. Most done wheat harvesting. About three weeks late this year.

5th. At home most all day on the pond reading. My eye rather bad. Could not sleep for the mosquitoes. Commenced sleeping in the mill.

Not so bad there. Thunder storm and rain.

6th. Went to Port Ryersee and broached the staff about their wood all day. They commenced rafting stacks of timber some 100 feet low.

7th. Started the mill a little while in the evening. Received a letter from Fanny containing the death of her father dated June 24th.

8th. Pit wheel qudion [quoin - corner stone?] loose. Commenced fastening that.

9th. Finished the qudion and started the mill. At work till 3 o'clock in the morning. Midnight dark and cloudy. Mill work good.

10th. Ground some wheat first. Leony here. Shot five woodcocks.

11th. I shot a large crane with my rifle and ground 15 wheat gusts today.

12th. Cloudy and cool. Writing to Fanny. My eye pain me much but almost directly after got quite well. At home all the afternoon, principally with Archy Steinhoff.

13th. Very busy gusting wheat. 9/10 yd. Flour $5 per 100.

14th. Finished furrowing the stones. Glad of it. Shot a very large crane with my rifle. Thunder storm.

15th. Very busy. Grow above 20 gusts, most of them small and some new rye wet. Wheat gust. Wet in the morning. Helped easure lumber.

16th. Rather poorly sick, swimmy and quite dread work today. Managed to keep on till night. Very tired and weak. Could not sleep.

17th. Not any better. Ground little more than a hundred bails of wheat. Most little lots. Great deal of bother with them. Some London porter gave 2/6 yd per common glass bottle for it. Have a little better appetite. Went to bed tired and poorly. Rather cool in the evening.

BACK HOME?

[August] 18th. Commenced to work the last day in Canada. This is the worst time for gusting of all the year. Rather poorly but better than I was yesterday. Much worse in the afternoon. Left off work at four o'clock and went to bed with the chill and the ague. No sleep.

19th. Sunday. Better in the morning. Went up the pond in the boat. Fever and chill came on worst in the afternoon. No sleep all night.

20th. Monday. Went stone dressing a little while. Chills on about noon. Very violent. My head dreadful bad with the fever. Hardly sensible. Mrs Adis bathed it with Camphine.

21st. Very weak. Broke the fever. Continued taking the choligog [medicine].

22nd. Had some port wine. $1 per bottle. Much better all day.

23rd. Poorly and very weak. About home all day and sometimes in the mill.

24th. About the same. Packed up most of my things and made my bed.

25th. Walked to Simcoe. Bade farewell to my Simcoe friends. Had dinner with Mr Waters. Rode home. Mr Carey had someone run the new mill.

26th. Miss Woolnough and Alack Coleman here. Went home with Alexa. The last day - at Marr's hollow. Left them at Windham.

27th. Up early and in the mill in the midst of flouring. Gave Mr Key ½ crown to carry me and my luggage to Port Dover. Pretty golly [a present] received from Mr Adis and $120 balance of wages. Left the mill at 10 o'clock at dinner and supper at Alexander Freres and put up the flower seeds with H Learey. About with him most all day in the evening. I was with Isabella Steinhoff for about six hours. Bid her farewell at 10 o'clock and got on board the ship The Plough Boy... H Learey on board... I went to my berth. I left the sweet shores of Canada at midday.

At this point what remains of the diary, just a page, becomes illegible, and the tantalising final fragments of his story are left untold. The journey home would probably have taken around two months and his family should have been overjoyed to see him. When I first read William Young's account, I thought his journey was one of necessity but now it looks more like a 'gap year', a chance to gain experience amongst the largely European settlers in that part of the New World. The conditions there were tough, the winters harsh and only the strongest survived. But for Young it must have been an invaluable experience at a time when many people remained in the same part of the country all their lives. Mainly the rich availed themselves of comfortable travel, often taking a few select servants with them. For Young this much more basic trip would have opened his eyes to new methods and new technology (such as the Niagara suspension bridge). As such, he could have brought these ideas back home with him, surely improving the lives of those at Cotchford Farm and nearby.

William Young has shown himself, through his diaries, to be amongst the hardest-working young men, who could be relied upon for all manner of tasks from stone-dressing to looking after crops. His care and precision must have made him much in demand and, when he apparently left Canada in August 1855 at the age of just twenty-four, it would have been a great loss. His family should have welcomed home a loving son (minus a few teeth!) who was more than capable of taking over the farm from his father when that time came, and no doubt equipped with new skills learned in Canada. His precision in all things financial and fascination with how things worked might well have made him a good engineer: consider his account of the Niagara suspension bridge and his understanding of agricultural markets and stone-dressing. While we may take issue with some of his shooting targets, this was a world accustomed to hunting and shooting, and whilst he worked quite extraordinarily hard, occasional fun and partying was interspersed with the graft.

No doubt about it, in his quiet way, Young was among England's finest, and quite a role model for other young men of the period. His diary provides a tantalising glimpse into both nineteenth-century travel half way across the world and frontier life on Lake Erie in an unforgiving climate.

But the story ends with a surprise. I have been unable to find out what happened to William Young after his departure from Canada. He does not seem to have returned to Cotchford Farm, and it is worth noting that he does not even appear there in the 1851 census, even before his journey to the New World. At that time, whilst in touch with his family, he was probably working at a location elsewhere in England, possibly because there was not enough work to justify his existence on his father's farm. This is perhaps suggested by the diary's references to the village of Cowden.

But in 1857, Henry Young, William's father sold the farm.

On WEDNESDAY, the 7th OCTOBER, 1857, at Levereux Hill Cowden ; the Live and Dead Farming Stock and Effects of Mr. W. Hollands, quitting the Farm.

On FRIDAY, the 9th OCTOBER, 1857, at " Haylands," Lingfield ; the excellent Milch Cow, Meadow Hay, a few Farming Implements, and Household Furniture of Mrs. Jackson, the estate being sold.

On MONDAY and TUESDAY, the 5th and 6th days of OCTOBER, at Scotchford Farm, Hartfield ; capital true Sussex and other bred Stock, excellent Cart Horses, Farming Implements, Household Furniture, Brewing and Dairy Utensils, and Effects of Mr. Henry Young, retiring from business.

On MONDAY and TUESDAY, 12th and 13th OCTOBER, at Bolebrooke Farm, Hartfield ; very superior Live and Dead Farming Stock, capital Agricultural Implements, Brewing and Dairy

Sussex Agricultural Express, Saturday. 29 August 1857

SCOTCHFORD FARM, HARTFIELD, SUSSEX.

MR. SMITH

IS instructed by the Proprietor, Mr. Hy. Young, who is retiring from Business, TO SELL BY AUCTION, upon the premises, on Monday, the 5th day of October, 1857, at 11 for 12 exact time,—

The whole of the well bred true Sussex STOCK, viz., five fine in-calf cows, a barren, 3 2-years old heifers (two in-calf), 6 fine yearling steers and heifers, 4 weaned calves, 4 excellent working oxen, 4 and 5-years old, a well bred 2-years old Sussex bull, 5 very excellent young cart horses, a capital brown nag gelding, 5 years old, quiet and good in harness, 2 sows in pig, a fine young boar, 4 store hogs, and 6 shuts.

FARMING IMPLEMENTS include 3 good 6 and 3 inch wheel waggons, 4 manure carts, roller, 9 horse and drag harrows, 6 ploughs, a nearly new patent chaff cutter, 5 trace and 3 quiler harnesses, a turnip cutter, about 3,000 10 feet hop poles and various small articles.

A few lots of Furniture, Brewing, Dairy, and Washing Utensils.

May be viewed on the morning of sale, and catalogues had, in due time at the inns in the neighbourhood, and at the Office of the AUCTIONEER, Eastgrinstead.

Sussex Agricultural Express, Saturday. 26 September 1857

William Fitt Cordery of Hazely in the Parish of Twyford aforesaid Farmer and Robert Archer Davis of Basingstoke in the said County Timber Merchant the Executors.

YOUNG Henry.

Effects under £2,000.

31 August. The Will with a Codicil of Henry Young formerly of Cotchford Farm in the Parish of Hartfield and late of Forest-row in the Parish of East Grinstead both in the County of **Sussex** Farmer deceased who died 28 June 1858 at Forest-row aforesaid was proved at **Lewes** by the oaths of John Payne of Crowborough Mills in the Parish of Withyham in the said County Miller Orpha Young of East Grinstead aforesaid Widow the Relict and Spencer Young of East Grinstead aforesaid Farmer the Son the Executors.

YOUNG James.

Effects under £6,000.

4 March. The Will of James Young late of Catterick in the County of **York** Gentleman deceased who died 29 July 1857 at Hurworth in the County of Durham was proved at **York** by the oaths of Isaac Thompson of Headingley in the Parish of Leeds in the said County of York Gentleman and Robinson Watson of Stockton in the said County of Durham Merchant the Executors.

YOUNG James.

Effects under £600.

27 May. The Will of James Young late of Twyford in the County of **Southampton** Yeoman deceased who died 27 October 1857 at Twyford aforesaid was proved at **Winchester** by the oath of Elizabeth Young of Twyford aforesaid Spinster the Sister and the sole Executrix.

YOUNG James.

Effects under £600.

16 September. The Will of James Young late of 7 Rye Croft-street Gloucester in the County of **Gloucester** Master Mariner deceased who died on or about 4 October 1857 at Sea was proved at the

Henry Young's will 1858

One might have expected him to pass it to his eldest son. But he did not. And when Henry died shortly afterwards in 1858, there is no mention of William Young. Had they become estranged or had William somehow become lost along the way? We do not know at present, and perhaps the author's puzzlement can now be understood. William Young's death at an early age cannot be ruled

Henry Young grave monument in St Swithun Church burial ground, East Grinstead, Sussex, England

Henry Young grave monument: legible names and details

full name	burial date	age	birth date
Henry Young	1858	72	1786
Orpah Young	1866	77	1789

The record of Henry and Orpah Young's grave

out. An atmosphere of sadness around the sale of the farm without an heir can be imagined. Did Henry die a disappointed man? We may never know.

The circumstances surrounding the certain death of Brian Jones of the Rolling Stones are also open to conjecture. The impact of Winnie-the-Pooh's global fame on Christopher Robin's mental health is a curious counterpoint to the author's success, just as the same syndrome affected author Kenneth Grahame's son even more acutely as a result of the publication of *The Wind in the Willows* (1908). William Young may have disappeared, but his diary, only quoted in part here, bequeaths a unique legacy in the form of a first-person account of life in mid-nineteenth-century Canada.

There is of course more to discover. How did the diary get back to England? Did it return with William or was it sent back with his belongings after an early death abroad? It makes sense to me that my aunt obtained the diary from Brighton because one of William Young's successors lived nearby and may have disposed of it as unwanted.

Is there an old grave somewhere under a shady oak in a Sussex country churchyard, quiet and unvisited? I certainly hope so.

The 14th Century Village church of Saint Andrews in the village of
Alfriston on the Sussex Downs

Gender:	Male
Baptism Date:	31 Jul 1831
Baptism Place:	Worth, Sussex, England
Father:	Henry Young
Mother:	Orpha
FHL Film Number:	0919105-6, 0416753

Record of William Young's birth

ACKNOWLEDGEMENTS

I WOULD LIKE to thank all those who have provided me with assistance for this book, especially Lord Ian Strathcarron and his team at Unicorn Publishing Group whose professionalism and attention to detail was of very great benefit; also, members of the Hartfield History Society who have provided me with useful additional information, as did the previous owner of Cotchford Farm, Alistair Johns.

This book is dedicated to my wife, Eithne, who has made some useful suggestions as well as putting up with endless annoyances in relation to the production of this volume.

APPENDIX 1
SOME NOTES ON THE TOWNS MENTIONED

BUFFALO CITY

Buffalo is the second largest city in the US state of New York and the largest in the western half of the state. As of 2018, the population was 256,304. It is the county seat of Erie County and a major gateway for commerce and travel across the Canada-United States border, forming part of the bi-national Buffalo-Niagara region.

The Buffalo area was inhabited prior to the seventeenth century by the Native American Iroquois tribe and later by French settlers. The city grew significantly in the nineteenth and twentieth centuries as a result of immigration, the construction of the Erie Canal and rail transportation, and its close proximity to Lake Erie. This growth provided access to an abundance of fresh water and an ample trade route to the Mid-Western United States, while grooming its economy for the grain, steel and automobile industries that dominated in the twentieth century. Since the city's economy relied heavily on manufacturing, de-industrialisation in the latter half of the twentieth century led to a steady decline in population. While some manufacturing activity remains, Buffalo's economy has switched to service industries with a greater emphasis on healthcare, research and higher education, which emerged following the Great Recession of the 1920s.

Buffalo is on the eastern shore of Lake Erie, at the head of the Niagara River, sixteen miles south of Niagara Falls. Its early use of electric power led to the nickname 'The City of Light'. The city is also famous for Joseph Ellicott's urban planning and layout, an extensive system of parks designed by Frederick Law Olmsted and significant architectural works. Its culture blends north-eastern and Mid-Western traditions, with annual festivals including the Taste of Buffalo food festival and the Allentown Arts Festival, two professional sports teams (the Buffalo Bills and the Buffalo Sabres) and a thriving and progressive music and arts scene.

PORT DOVER

Prior to the War of 1812, this community was known as Dover Mills. It is the southern terminus for Ontario Highway 6, located 480km or 300 miles to the south of the northern Ontario community of McKerrow. This highway stretches northward as a two-lane, undivided highway until the traffic flow increases to four lanes shortly after departure from Caledonia. In addition to allowing Port Dover residents direct access to the city of Hamilton, it also briefly merges with Highway 403 to allow access to the Royal Botanical Gardens and other locations on to Toronto.

The second largest of the communities in Norfolk County, Ontario, Port Dover had a population of 6,161 at the time of the 2016 Census. The majority of residents speak English, with 285 people speaking languages other than English or French. Most were born in Canada, although 515 residents were born in Europe in addition to 10 African-born residents, 70 US-born residents and 70 who were born in Asia.

At least 4,331 individuals and/or families are interred at Port Dover Cemetery on the Blue Line Road, including a locally well-known novelist, John Raymond Kaiser. The cemetery is a United Empire Loyalist cemetery, with veterans from the War of 1812 and other conflicts that Canada was involved in. Due to the changing Canadian economic climate, a storage space for cremated remains was installed on the premises in 2011.

PORT RYERSE

Port Ryerse is a fishing hamlet in Norfolk County, Ontario, south-west of Port Dover. Many residents of south-western Ontario rent cottages and fish for pleasure there during the summer months (Victoria Day to mid-October).

Many residents live there year-round, and most drive to Port Dover or Simcoe to purchase groceries and other goods, although Port Ryerse did boast a historic general store until it burned down in September 2004. There are still handmade soap, bath and folk art shops in the community. It lies at the mouth of Young's Creek (popular with trout fishermen) and empties into Long Point Bay. Nearby is Hay Creek Conservation Area, that can be used year-round and is suitable for hiking, walking, cycling, cross-country skiing and snowshoeing.

Port Ryerse was founded by Lieutenant-Colonel Samuel Ryerse, brother of Colonel Joseph Ryerson and uncle of Egerton Ryerson. Its harbour was important for shipping cargo from Norfolk County across the lake, although it declined significantly around the 1880s due to the advent of the railway.

Samuel Ryerse was a United Empire Loyalist who fought with the British during the American Revolution and arrived in Upper Canada in 1794 where he received 3,000 acres of land. He built a grist mill at the mouth of Young's Creek and a settlement grew up around it. Ryerse remained involved with the military as Lieutenant of the County of Norfolk and was also the chairman of the Court of Quarter Sessions.

The mill was burned by American troops in 1814 during the War of 1812. In later years, two new grist mills were built at the same location but both burned down (in 1860 and in 1890). A brick schoolhouse was built in 1871.

Port Ryerse is also the birthplace of John Edward Brownlee, the Premier of the province of Alberta during the Roaring Twenties and through the early years of the Great Depression. John Brownlee had one sister, Maude, born 12 September 1888. The Brownlees lived in the general store building, where John spent the happiest years of his childhood; he much preferred his parents' books, their political discussions with neighbours and details of their business, to life outside the store. In one anecdote, the village children, displeased with his serious temperament, threw him into Lake Erie. By the age of seven, John was assisting at the store, performing such tasks as mixing butter from the different dairies with which his father dealt to produce a standardised blend.

A public elementary school called Port Ryerse School was in operation from the nineteenth century until the 1950s. Both Caucasian and African-Canadian students were photographed attending the school on 14 September 1898 along with their teacher, a Miss A. Exelby.

The Memorial Anglian Church Cemetery is located in the hamlet, where at least twenty-six individuals and/or families are buried.

At least 194 different bird species were discovered here between 1875 and 2019, including the passenger pigeon, the indigo bunting and the northern cardinal.

In 2001, Haldimand-Norfolk was dissolved into two separate

single-tier counties. Port Ryerse became part of the newly formed County of Norfolk. .

SIMCOE

Simcoe was founded in 1795 by Lieutenant-Governor John Graves Simcoe. Initially, the settlement consisted of two distinct areas: Birdtown, named by William Bird who arrived in the early 1800s, and the Queensway, which grew up around Aaron Culver's sawmill and grist mill in the 1820s. The post office opened in 1829 and was called Simcoe. In 1837, the village became the seat of government of the then Talbot District.

A historical plaque adds that Lieutenant-Governor Simcoe gave land to Aaron Culver in 1795 on condition that he would build mills there; a hamlet had formed by 1812, but was burned down by American troops in 1814. Between 1819 and 1823 Culver laid out a village; streets were surveyed from 1835–6. Simcoe was also instrumental in helping to end the slave trade in Canada and also introducing trial by jury.

Records from 1846 indicate that the settlement was far from any major roads and had little communication with areas outside of Brantford, and that a stone courthouse and jail had already been built; the courthouse would be destroyed by fire in 1863 and rebuilt. There were three churches: Methodist, Baptist and Congregationalist. A weekly newspaper is published here, The Long Point Advocate. About this time, the population was around 1,400. The post office was receiving mail daily. This settlement contained the offices of the Judge of District Court, Sheriff, Clerk of Peace, Inspector of Licenses, Crown Lands Agent, District Clerk, Treasurer, Clerk of District Court, Deputy Clerk of Crown and the Superintendent of Schools. Already operating were two grist mills, two sawmills, a brewery, two distilleries, a foundry, a fulling mill, nine stores, six taverns, two druggists, a bank (Gore) and many tradesmen. In 1850 the population was around 1,600 and in the same year Simcoe became the county seat of Norfolk County. The population had increased to 2,100 by 1869 and two banks had opened.

Simcoe was incorporated as a town in 1878, and had its own town council and mayor until 31 December 2000. In 2001, the town and all other municipalities within the Regional Municipality of Haldimand-Norfolk were dissolved and the region divided into two single-tier municipalities, with city status but known as counties: a strange arrangement. Simcoe now forms Ward 5 of Norfolk County, a very different place from the basic facilities offered in William Young's time.

.

APPENDIX 2

THE FOLLOWING ARE copies of original pages from William Young's diary. Note the closely written script and detailed, confident hand. Because of its age, not all of its fifty-odd pages are entirely legible, frustratingly so towards the end, when we especially want to know what happened to William. Spelling remains a problem and where in doubt, I have opted for consistency and left as written.

The diary contains references to 'gusting' in relation to stonework. While neither I nor the Stone Federation of Great Britain could positively identify this, their technical expert suggests that it may be 'an old term used in a local area, not nationwide and would refer to getting rid of the surplus before tackling the more refined work. Although large quantities of stone were being used, due to the high cost of transport it could be very much a local business with its own jargon'. (2021)

1854

Thursday 29th June Started from Scotland at ¼ past 6 Oclock and arriv'd at Edenbridge Station at ½ past 7 train started for London at ¼ past 8 it rain'd all the way from Hartfield to London paid 1/ from London Bridge to Euston Square paid 2/7 from E B to L Bridge walk'd about the west end in the Afternoon and Evening and came home very tired at Brownlow place Dalston stay'd there all night

30th got up at 5 Oclock and walk'd to Euston Sq train started at 7 a m and arrived at Liverpool at 45 M past 7 P M. Paid for fare 16/9 by 3rd Class pass'd the time away pretty comfortable.

July 1 Stopt at 20 Spitalfields nearly all day except a little while in the evening took a walk to some of the docks and saw very little except sailors and girls.

2 Sunday very poorly all day walk'd a little way in the evening.

3 a great deal worse laid down nearly all day took some medicine and got better towards Even

4 a great deal better went to the Parisian Gallery of Anatomy saw 300 Anatomical Models and heard a good lecture and learnt much.

temperance the D[r] was drunk at the time but talk
pretty sencible there were a great majority in favour
of a prohibatary law a good attendance 2 horses E
the first time I walked with a girl arm in arm since I left
18th Snow storm continued all day with wind from north
I kept at home all day rather dull no one here.
19 very cold clear and frosty Wheat gate froze up continuity
began to think E— was better than Canada
20th cold clear nowind cleaning the dinnt room out
21 rather warmer at work on the pond in the morning
cutting down wood (about this time doubts about religion
22 warmer with some more snow very busy
23rd warmer weather had the tooth ake in the night — not much
doing in the Mills pretty good sleighing saw logs came in thick
Prices of grain } Wheat 11/4 [th] Buck Wheat 6/ Corn 7/ Oats 4/6
Flour 4 ß Buck Wheat 3 ß Corn Meal 2 ß Midg[s] Chop 12/ 7th
Bran & Shorts 5/ 7th Midls 13/ Corn Flour 20/ Buck W[t] Bran 5/
hay from 14 ß to 20 ß per ton potatoe 4/ 7th turnips 2/ 7th
Beef 5 cents per [lb] Mutton from 7 to 10 cents Geese each 2/ to 3/
Tire wood 1 ß per cord when cut Slabs and edgin 1/ 7th per load
24 Sunday Simcoe Mills Burnt down Belongin to Riche
Ford & Jones[t] 12 000 Bus of Wheat destroyed besides other
corn & flour and a great quantity of flour Whiskey
warm Weather. Mr & H Leamy came in the morning at home all
the morning and all went to the fire in the afternoon

BIBLIOGRAPHY/FILMOGRAPHY

British Agricultural Revolution, en.wikipedia.org/wiki/ Agricultural Revolution. Accessed 16/02/18.

Canadian town notes sourced from Wikipedia, August 2019, and as adapted.

Gravestone Photographic Resource, 2018.

http//w.w.w.the shipslist.com/ships/lines/shtml Tapscott Line of Packets, 26/06/18.

Hardy R. (director), *The Wicker Man*, British Lion Films, GB 1973.

Johnson L, *Lake Erie Hides Secrets of 2000 Shipwrecks* (2017), http://rockthelake. com/buzz/2017/10/lake-erie-hides-secrets-2000-shipwrecks. 14/08/19.

Kent History and Library Centre, ref QM/SRc/1596/14 as listed in the National Archives.

McGreevy E.E., *Chaos at Sea: The Mutiny Aboard The William Tapscott*, Glucksman Ireland House, New York University, 2017.

Mormon Immigration Index, https://saintsbysea.lib.byu.edu.mii/ voyage/434. 21/08/19.

Probatesearch.service.gov.uk 2018.

Sussex Agricultural Express, Saturday, 29 August 1857

Sussex Agricultural Express, Saturday, 26 September 1857.

Sutton, C.N., *Historical Notes of Withyham*, A.K. Baldwin (Tunbridge Wells) 1902 and as reprinted by Alpha Editions (2019).